SpringerBriefs in Psychology

SpringerBriefs in Theoretical Advances in Psychology

SpringerBriefs in Theoretical Advances in Psychology will be an extension from the currently renovated Annals of Theoretical Psychology in the direction of bringing short, single (or multiple) authored theoretical advancements across all areas of psychology to the international audience. The focus is on the development of innovative theoretical approaches and their discussion. The Series will have a clearly defined international and interdisciplinary focus – even if it remains within the discipline of psychology.

Featuring compact volumes of 100 to 115 pages, each Brief in the Series is meant to provide a clear, visible, and multi-sided recognition of the theoretical efforts of scholars around the world. It is targeted to researchers, graduate students, and professionals in Post-BA level psychology, education, anthropology, and sociology.

Briefs are published as part of the Springer's eBook collection, with millions of users worldwide. In addition, Briefs are available for individual print and electronic purchase.

More information about this subseries at http://www.springer.com/series/14346

David Torres Irribarra

A Pragmatic Perspective of Measurement

Springer

David Torres Irribarra
Escuela de Psicología
Pontificia Universidad Católica de Chile
Santiago, Chile

ISSN 2192-8363 ISSN 2192-8371 (electronic)
SpringerBriefs in Psychology
ISSN 2511-395X ISSN 2511-3968 (electronic)
SpringerBriefs in Theoretical Advances in Psychology
ISBN 978-3-030-74024-5 ISBN 978-3-030-74025-2 (eBook)
https://doi.org/10.1007/978-3-030-74025-2

This Springer imprint is published by the registered company Springer Nature Switzerland AG
The registered company address is: Gewerbestrasse 11, 6330 Cham, Switzerland

In memory of my grandfather,
Raúl Irribarra Opazo, who through his actions taught me the measure of what a man can be.

Series Editors' Preface for David Torres Irribarra *A Pragmatic Perspective of Measurement*

Mathematical Thinking, Social Practices, and the Locus of Science in Psychology

The origins of modern psychology are inevitably entwined with the introduction of naturalistic quantitative methods in the nineteenth century. In fact, the endeavour of social sciences as a whole is indebted to the impressive expansion of the natural scientific worldview during that century. By embracing formalization as a privileged gateway to knowledge by the dawn of the nineteenth century, the natural sciences showed the societal benefits of mathematically explaining and predicting events of the natural world. This is the context for the expansion of formal methods from the natural sciences to the human sciences, which became an imperative. The historical process of moving towards the natural scientific worldview during that century was promoted by the doubter Immanuel Kant (who did not expect psychology ever to reach a state of mathematically precise science) and Johann Friedrich Herbart after him (who tried to mathematize psychology in the first half of the nineteenth century). Herbart, a capital figure of the rising "new psychology", warned in 1822: "Mathematics is the ruling science of our times; its victories grow daily though quietly; whoever is not *for* it, one day will have it *against* them" (Herbart, 1822, p.105, our translation, italics in the original). One generation later, Herbart's exhortation led Gustav T. Fechner to introduce the measurement of psychophysiological processes and inaugurate psychophysics. One generation after that, Wilhelm Wundt proposed *experimental psychology* as a research program that featured psychophysics in a broader field that included the entire field of traditional psychology, but with natural scientific methods within. Following the large fight on the German grounds between *Naturwissenschaften* and *Geisteswissenschaften* over the nineteenth century, psychology was left as an impaired victim in between—crying out for mathematics and unable to fit it with the complexities of the human soul.

Not only contemporary psychology, but the whole endeavour of social sciences is in a sense captured by the expansion of the natural scientific worldview during that century. Once the formalization of natural phenomena was embraced as the gateway to true knowledge by the dawn of the nineteenth century, the natural sciences had shown the powerful intellectual benefits for general knowledge. The history of chemistry—another discipline that was predicted by Kant never become a science—successfully became so through multi-level expansion of its language into a state where different tasks could be fitted with different—formalized or not—purposes (Valsiner, 2012, chapter 9). Some aspects of mathematics that were fitting the seeming usefulness of developing psychology were adapted in the beginning of the twentieth century. This entailed the creation of mathematical statistics based on the British eugenic world views. In contrast, many other parallel streams of mathematics were left out of these expansions in the social sciences and have remained so until today (covered in Rudolph, 2013).

The main rationale for the limited borrowing of mathematics in the beginning of the twentieth century was the pragmatist idea of predicting and controlling events of the natural world. In this context, the spread of formal methods—but not their axiomatic origins—from natural sciences to the human sciences was turned from a possibility to an imperative. This was the societal message of Auguste Comte's *positive philosophy* that flourished from the 1830s onward. When a particular framework of thinking become a social imperative instituted in a given science by means of institutional forces of curriculae, evaluation systems, and career promotion rules—science ends, or at least becomes stagnating. We can feel that in our twenty-first century.

The opposition to mathematization of psychology curiously supported the limited mathematization trends in the twentieth century. The introduction of mathematical tools to develop a new psychology was far from being accepted without contest. In his 1894 *Ideas for a Descriptive and Analytic Psychology*', Wilhelm Dilthey argued that in the divide between natural and human sciences, not only should psychology belong to the latter, but that it should serve as a foundation to the rest of the human sciences. In this spirit, psychology should put the *understanding* of meaning over causal *explanation* (Dilthey, 2010). This tension has been accompanied by a distrust toward the formal measurement of psychological phenomena, arguably related to an inadequacy of natural scientific methods to approach the nature of psychic life.

Posing this question was legitimate then—as it is now (Salvatore, 2016). The difficulties in explaining the unique features of psychic phenomena with the causal principles that rule the spatio-temporal dimensions of matter simply bypasses the specific open-systemic nature of all psychological phenomena. Any effort to predict these mathematically would require a new—open-systemic—mathematics. This has not yet been derived. This gap leads to questioning of the use of closed-systems (General Linear Model) mathematics in psychology leads to an epistemological question—viz., the *fitness between method and psychological matters*—or even to an ontological one—viz., what precisely is meant by psychological matter and its susceptibility to be described.

Since posing the question on the adequacy of quantification in psychology implies doing epistemology—which to mainstream psychology means "going back" to philosophical times—this kind of inquiry has encountered massive resistance within the discipline. Wundt's intellectual offspring seem to have forgotten the metaphysical and epistemological shoulders their sophisticated methodological practices stand on. Far from a useless pre-scientific activity, a conceptual examination of our beliefs is mandatory in research if we are to find methods that are faithful to phenomena. As mainstream psychologists become more immersed in psychological *scientism* and fall off from *scientific* psychology, they deem historical and conceptual analyses to be irrelevant and related to anti-scientific practices. They seem to be following Wittgenstein's advice to understand his *Tractatus Logico-Philosophicus* to the letter: "[One] must so to speak throw away the ladder, after [one] has climbed up on it" (Wittgenstein, 1922, p. 6.54). Psychologists do not seem to remember that their predecessors needed metaphysics to nuance the omniscience of mathematics. The rapid adoption of the scientific method during the nineteenth century seems to have overturned the entirety of human sciences even before a conceptual clarification of its scope and limits was properly made. However, as with any untreated issue, the discussion opens up again from time to time.

Two hundred years after Herbart made his assessment, quantitative methodology—but not elaborated mathematical science—lies unquestioned at the core of psychology curricula around the world. Arguments from outside the field have done little to temper a seeping trend obsessed with the use of still unfamiliar mathematical tools as a foundation to transform psychology into a so-called "*real science*". In this sense, opponents of naturalistic psychology have failed to show the reasons to abandon or to reformulate the use of mathematical tools. A major revolt against quantitative methods in the 1960s ended up sealing a friendly armistice between the quantitative and the qualitative, as if polarizing things would solve the issue. In this truce, the former would allow in "qualitative" techniques as an alternative and the latter would adopt the metatheoretical principles of the natural sciences; namely, rigor, replicability and objectivity. Qualitatively oriented psychologists failed to realize that the discussion they were involved in is epistemological in nature, not narrowly those of methods. Consequently, "qualitative methods" became more and more rigid, and they did not lead into a fruitful discussion about the adequacy of methods in psychology. Again—an opportunity has been missed—instead of "mixed methods" that are nowadays hailed as a solution we need *coordinated methods* that share relevant methodological unity (Valsiner, 2017)

The current exponential growth of computational capacities and the internet have triggered renewed and powerful forms of scientism in modern societies (Haack, 2017). Under "scientism" we understand the ideological conviction that only the natural scientific methods produce genuine knowledge, while "non-scientific fields are ripe for colonization by the sciences or else are illegitimate, best abandoned altogether" (Haack, 2017, p.8). Darwinitis, neuromania (Gabriel, 2017; Tallis, 2011) as well as big data are among its manifestations in contemporary psychology. Laplace's demon seems to be brought back to life once again, but now with unlimited computational capacities fed by stocks of information provided by internet users. This situation seems particularly dangerous for a field that seems obsessively concerned with methods but unresponsive to the nature of its matter.

The contemporary ideology of scientism has turned fallible, open-ended scientific inquiry into a cookie-cutter application of methods (irrespective of quantitative or qualitative approaches). More than susceptible, psychology seems to be completely indifferent to colonization by big-data and the techno-biological views of humankind.

Therein lies the importance of David Torres Irribarra's present treatise. In his book, the author undertakes the issue of psychological measurement and the conditions for quantification of psychic phenomena. This exercise is just as valuable as it is unusual. It does not correspond to postmodern criticisms to the entire enterprise of quantification in psychology. As mentioned, this type of "everything must be thrown away" position has proven to be unable to detain the uses and misuses of mathematics in psychology. Furthermore, David Torres Irribarra presents a brief but exhaustive revision of the main theoretical approaches to measurement (see Chap. 2). On the one hand, he provides an insight into the relationship between the properties of measuring scales and those of measured phenomena. On the other hand, he presents methodological choices (variable types being nominal, ordinal, continuous, etc.) as authored and designed with specific purposes. This exposition is in sharp contrast with usual methodology handbooks, where such definitions are simply presented as bearing an authoritative component. After a useful introduction to American Pragmatism (Chap. 1), David Torres Irribarra offers a pragmatist interpretation of measurement procedures (Chaps. 3 and 4) where they are presented as part of social activity and therefore oriented toward a larger social goal. Finally, in Chap. 5, the author contrasts his pragmatist interpretation to existing perspectives on measurement.

We hope this work contributes to reveal the philosophical underpinnings of current measurement theories in psychology, education and the social sciences. A renewal of the epistemological discussion on the uses and limitations of mathematical tools in these disciplines seems indispensable.

Santiago, Chile
Aalborg, Denmark
February 2021

Carlos Cornejo
Jaan Valsiner

References

Dilthey, W. (2010). *Selected works, Vol. II Introduction to the human sciences* (R. A. Makkreel & F. Rodi, Eds.). Princeton University Press.

Gabriel, M. (2017). *I'm not a brain: philosophy of mind for the twenty-first century*. Polity Press.

Haack, S. (2017). *Scientism and its discontents*. Rounded Globe.

Herbart, J. F. (1890). *Sämtliche Werke*, 5th volume (K. Kehrbach, Ed.). Hermann Beyer & Söhne [Originally published in 1822].

Rudolph, L. (Ed.) (2013). *Qualitative mathematics for the social sciences*. London: Routledge.
Salvatore, S. (2016). Commentary 2: the past and the history of psychology. In S. H. Klempe & R. Smith (Eds.), *Centrality of history for theory construction in psychology* (pp. 235–240). Springer.
Tallis, R. (2011). *Aping mankind: Neuromania, Darwinitis and the misrepresentation of humanity*. Acumen.
Valsiner, J. (2012). *A guided science: History of psychology in the mirror of its making*. New Brunswick, NJ: Transaction Publishers.
Valsiner J. (2017). *From methodology to methods in human psychology*. New York: SpringerBriefs
Wittgenstein, L. (1922). *Tractatus logico-philosophicus*. London: Kegan Paul, Trench, Trubner & Co.

Preface

Measurement has been for a long time a ubiquitous activity, one that is associated with the production of valuable information that we can use in order to make decisions in many domains of our lives (Duncan 1984). The prototypical associations to what it means to measure an attribute have historically been connected with physical attributes, such that we tend to think of rulers that measure distance and scales that measure weight as prime examples of this practice. However, in the last century or so, the social sciences have striven to actively engage in this activity, attempting to *measure* a wide variety of social and psychological concepts (Michell 1999; Woolf 1961). This endeavour has been successful at the very least to the extent that it is no longer strange to hear, and accept, that psychologists can measure a person's intelligence or that educators can measure students' level of mathematical knowledge or writing ability.

However, despite the successful adoption of the idea that measurement is not activity limited to mass, distance, and other physical attributes, but also an activity that can be conducted on social and psychological attributes, it is not always clear how this jump from the physical to the psycho-social has changed the way in which we understand measurement. Do we mean exactly the same thing when we claim to measure length as when we claim to measure anxiety? If not, what is the difference? Should we trust in thermometers in the same way in which we trust personality tests? Are there limits to what can be measured? These are central questions that raise issues regarding the possibility of conducting measurement at all in the social sciences, the way in which the measurement procedures and outcomes can be interpreted, and the role that measurement plays in the development of social and psychological theories. Many scholars have raised these and other issues, often criticizing the use of the concept of measurement in the social sciences, and the reticence of social scientists to cope with these theoretical and philosophical questions about the definition and practice of measurement (Boring 1920; Borsboom 2005; Cliff 1992; Johnson 1936; Michell 2008a; Schönemann 1994; Trendler 2009).

The disconnect between the now common acceptance of measurement in the social sciences and simultaneous lack of attention to the theory on which the practice is predicated is nicely illustrated by Allport in the 1935 *Handbook of Social Psychology* where he states:

> The interest of American social psychologists in fact-collecting and statistical methods has resulted in a rapid advance in the empirical study of attitudes, with the result that *attitudes today are measured more successfully than they are defined.* [emphasis added] (p. 828)

These questions about the very possibility of measurement in the social sciences exist at the same time that the practice is widely accepted in society, serving as the basis for personnel selection, educational placement, and international comparisons. In this context, it is not an option to simply expect researchers, technicians, and consumers to stop what they are doing until we achieve a coherent and widely accepted basis for conducting psycho-social measurements. At the same time, it is not tenable to continue trusting implicitly in any claim of measurement of psycho-social concepts to the extent that some of these basic questions regarding the meaning and validity of the practice remain unanswered. This situation brings to mind Neurath's famous allegory (1973):

> We are like sailors who on the open sea must reconstruct their ship but are never able to start afresh from the bottom. Where a beam is taken away a new one must at once be put there, and for this the rest of the ship is used as support. In this way, by using the old beams and driftwood the ship can be shaped entirely anew, but only by gradual reconstruction. (p. 199)

This book, adapted from part of my doctoral dissertation, is presented in the spirit of a gradual effort for reconsidering—or reconstructing as the allegory has it—the ship of measurement in the social sciences. With this goal, *A Pragmatic Perspective on Measurement* addresses the definition of measurement question, presenting a conceptualization of the practice of measurement from the perspective of the pragmatic tradition in philosophy (Bacon 2012; James 1907/1995; Rorty 1999).

Santiago, Chile
November 2020

David Torres Irribarra

Contents

Chapter 1
Introduction

Let me start with an imaginary dialog between a researcher who recently finished a study on anxiety and a skeptic.

Researcher: As a part of my study I measured anxiety.
Skeptic: How exactly did you manage to do that?
Researcher: Well, I designed a questionnaire with five Likert-type questions, collected a lot of data, analyzed the results to ensure the quality of the instrument, and, after checking that everything was in order, I calculated an estimate of anxiety for each participant in the study.

The researcher seems to be following usual practice in psychology and the social sciences,[1] but the question remains, did the researcher *really* measure anxiety? When he says "I measured anxiety," the skeptic wonders whether she can place similar trust as she would place in the results of a speedometer or a thermometer gauge, or similar instances of measurement that have gained acceptance and respect broadly in our society. After all, as Van Fraassen (2008) points out:

> The term "measurement" is an endorsing term. If we call something a measurement, we imply that there is something correct or valuable in the way it yields a representation (even if on this particular occasion it went wrong). Measuring is an operation by which we can produce or gather information; and here "information" too has an endorsing sense. (p. 151)

The high regard for the label of *measurement* has increased over time due to the unparalleled success of measuring and modeling of the physical world, which Wigner (1960) described as *"the unreasonable effectiveness of mathematics in the*

[1] See, for example, Knapp and Mueller (2010) for an example on recommended guidelines for reviewers of manuscripts presenting measurement instruments.

D. Torres Irribarra, *A Pragmatic Perspective of Measurement*, SpringerBriefs in Psychology, https://doi.org/10.1007/978-3-030-74025-2_1

physical sciences"[2] (p. 222), and has made it so that *"in our own time, measurement means nothing if not precision and objectivity"* (Porter 1996, p. 23).

The social sciences have long aimed at replicating this success, and in this spirit have pursued the measurement of their attributes of interest. "Quality of life," "intelligence," "aptitude," "knowledge," "customer satisfaction," "job performance," "similarity," "utility," "prejudice," "well-being," "socio-economic status," and "social capital" are all examples of concepts that social scientists claim to have measured.

In the face of all these measurement claims, the emergence of a certain level of skepticism (cf. Johnson 1936; Trendler 2009) seems natural and healthy. Is there a limit at all to what can be measured? What does it mean to measure something? It is not clear how far we are willing to extend that concept.

Is a measure of the diagonal of a screen equivalent in trustworthiness to the measure of someone's mathematical ability? If the trust that the public places on measures in the social sciences relies on their connection to the notion of measurement in the physical sciences, and their results are used to make inferences and decisions about persons and public policies, then the clarification of the similarities and differences between measurement in the physical and the social realms is of central importance to adequately contextualize their relative advantages and limitations.

To address these concerns about the scope and limits of measurement scholars have attempted, since the beginnings of modern social sciences, to define a clear demarcation between measurement and non-measurement (Borsboom 2005; Campbell 1920; Mari 2003; Michell 1999; Savage 1970; Stevens 1946). Such a criterion would supposedly allow us to separate quackery and posturing from *real measurement*, by providing a way of testing which claims should enjoy the trust of the scientific community and public opinion. Some have looked for the key to defining the concept of measurement in the nature of the attributes that we purport to measure (Michell 2005), others have emphasized the methods that we must follow to achieve it (Krantz et al. 1971/2007; Mari 2000), and still others have even focused on its products (Dingle 1950; Speitel 1992). Despite their differences, most, if not all, of these efforts attempt to answer the question: What is the *true* and conclusive definition of measurement? I, too, have found myself tempted by this longing for that definition of measurement that will finally provide us with a clear-cut criterion. However, despite the many answers that can be found in the literature, I have come to think that the problem lies in formulating the question in this manner.

[2]Wigner recognizes that this effectiveness is a product of an historical development process: "It is true, of course, that physics chooses certain mathematical concepts for the formulation of the laws of nature, and surely only a fraction of all mathematical concepts is used in physics. It is true also that the concepts which were chosen were not selected arbitrarily from a listing of mathematical terms but were developed, in many if not most cases, independently by the physicist and recognized then as having been conceived before by the mathematician." (p. 229) yet he is still amazed by its results.

In this book, I would like to elaborate how pragmatism, a philosophical perspective that turns away from ahistorical accounts of knowledge, embracing instead "the role of *know-how*, *social practices*, and *human agency*" (Bernstein 2010, p. 9), can help us address questions about the definition and limits of measurement; and how in doing so it can challenge some deep-seated assumptions shared by most, if not all, of the alternative accounts of measurement cited above, so that we can think about it in a different, and hopefully more productive, way.

1.1 What Is Pragmatism?

In its colloquial sense, "pragmatic" is oftentimes associated with *practical* as being somehow devoid of, opposed to, or at least not requiring, theory. A clear example of this usage in the measurement literature can be found in Hand (2004, p. 53):[3]

> ... the pragmatic part is purely operational, and is simply an arbitrary aspect of the process of taking the measurement—arbitrary in the sense that other measurement procedures may adopt alternative pragmatic constraints.

This is not the sense in which I use the word in this book. I discuss how theory-building is one more of the many activities that humans engage in coping with the world, and how from a pragmatist's perspective, theories are powerful tools in their own right. In the sense used in this book, pragmatism is not evoked to say "we don't really need to think about theory."

A second informal use of the word "pragmatic" is to mean *expedient* or *convenient*, and somehow limited to a short-term perspective. Short-term consequences and applications can certainly be considered, but I want to emphasize that the pragmatist perspective described in this book does not restrict the focus to them. In any given issue there are interesting discussions to be had regarding uses and consequences in the long- and medium- versus the short-term, but a pragmatic attitude does not necessarily favor any of them in principle.

Finally, it is important to recognize that many people consider themselves to be practical or pragmatic. I do not pretend to be the arbiter of what is the correct use of the word or who gets to be in the "pragmatic club." However, in this book, I refer to pragmatism as the approach developed in the pragmatic tradition associated in its origins with Peirce (1878/2014), James (1907/1995), Dewey (1929/1960, 1920/2004), and more recently with the neo-pragmatism of Rorty (1982, 1999).

[3]In his treatment of what he calls "pragmatic measurement" Hand links it to operationalism, and although he explicitly decries the confusion between them, his treatment conflates them: "the results of any [unrestricted] transformation would define an equally legitimate, pragmatic measurement procedure. Of course, it would be a different procedure... so perhaps we should give the resulting variable a different name." (p. 57–58).

As with any other tradition, pragmatism is hardly monolithic, prompting Westbrook (2008, p.185) to characterize it "less as a well defined, tightly knit school of thought than as a loose, contentious family of thinkers who have always squabbled, and have sometimes been moved to disown one another." Throughout this book, I try to present the common or more distinctive elements of this tradition, and when appropriate I discuss which family members' interpretations I am favoring.

1.2 A Brief Overview of Some Pragmatist Ideas

1.2.1 The Primacy of Practice

Briefly speaking, pragmatism is a philosophical tradition that emphasizes that the meaning of an idea or concept can be characterized by the effects that it produces. This core idea was expressed by Peirce (1878/2014) in what is now known as the *pragmatic maxim*:

> Consider what effects, which might conceivably have practical bearings, we conceive the object of our concept to have. Then, our conception of these effects is the whole of our conception of the object. (p. 31)

The maxim directs our attention toward what James (1907/1995) called the *practical cash-value* of our ideas and theories in order to help us understand them and judge their worth. On the centrality of this currency Peirce (1878/2014) indicates that "we come down to what is tangible and practical, as the root of every real distinction of thought, no matter how subtle it may be; and there is no distinction of meaning so fine as to consist in anything but a possible difference of practice" (p. 30). This emphasis is a central thread that connects pragmatic thinkers, even though different members of the pragmatic family may advance different interpretations of what "tangible and practical" means (Bacon 2012).[4]

It is worth mentioning at this point that a kindred approach to meaning can also be found in Ludwig Wittgenstein's later work, where he discusses meaning as tied to use:

> The meaning of a phrase for us is characterized by the use we make of it. The meaning is not a mental accompaniment to the expression....—I want to play chess, and a man gives the white king a paper crown, leaving the use of the piece unaltered, but telling me that the crown has a meaning to him in the game, which he can't express by rules. I say: "as long as it doesn't alter

[4]Perhaps the clearest example of a divergence on this issue occurs between Peirce and James, where the latter interpreted the notion of "practical" to include moral, aesthetic, and religious concerns, while the former restricted it to experimental/observational terms (Bacon 2012; Rescher 2007).

> the use of the piece, it hasn't what I call a meaning." (Wittgenstein 1965, p. 65)

Even though he is not usually considered a pragmatist, Wittgenstein's work has been actively discussed and used by leading pragmatists such as Rorty (1979) and Putnam (1995), and the affinity of his work with some key pragmatic ideas has been often noted and discussed (e.g., Goodman 1998; Haack 1982; Hensley 2009; Margolis 2009). Because of this affinity, I avail myself of Wittgenstein's work throughout this book when arguing for a pragmatic perspective of measurement.

1.2.2 Fallibilism and Anti-skepticism

A second central aspect of the pragmatic tradition, going back to Peirce's article *Some Consequences of Four Incapacities* (1868), is the commitment to both fallibilism and anti-skepticism (Bacon 2012). To be a fallibilist means accepting that any belief can be subject to revision, no matter how entrenched or central to us; to put it bluntly, it means accepting that we can always be wrong about anything. Although this might seem to be courting utter skepticism, pragmatists explicitly distance themselves from this position, assuming an anti-skeptic position that means that "while any particular belief might, in the course of inquiry, be upset and overturned, they are unproblematically relied upon until reason to question them is given" (Bacon 2012, p. 20). This balancing act between fallibilism and anti-skepticism is rooted in Peirce's doctrine that "reasoning should not form a chain which is no stronger than its weakest link, but a cable whose fibers may be ever so slender, provided they are sufficiently numerous and intimately connected" (Peirce 1868, p. 141).

Bernstein (1998) argues that the impact of Peirce's doctrine expressed in his 1868 article can be seen almost a century later in the work of Sellars (1956). In his 1956 article "Empiricism and the Philosophy of Mind" Sellars states that "empirical knowledge, like its sophisticated extension, science, is rational, not because it has a *foundation* but because it is a self-correcting enterprise which can put *any* claim in jeopardy, though not *all* at once" (p. 300). The importance of the fallibilist and anti-skeptic stance for the pragmatic tradition is best summarized in the words of Putnam (1995):

> Pragmatists hold that *doubt* requires justification just as much as belief.... [and] that there are no metaphysical guarantees to be had that even our most firmly-held beliefs will never need revision. That one can be both fallibilistic *and* antisceptical is perhaps *the* basic insight of American Pragmatism. (p. 20–21)

1.2.3 Historical and Social Nature of Knowledge

Another strand of pragmatist thought is its rejection of an "ahistorical, transcendental, or metaphysical theory of truth" (Misak 2013, p. 3), and embracing instead "a nonfoundational self-corrective conception of human inquiry based upon an understanding of how human agents are formed by, and actively participate in shaping, normative social practices" (Bernstein 2010, p. x).

Pragmatist thinkers may differ on the impact of the social and historical nature of knowledge, varying from those who follow in Peirce's footsteps by formulating a pragmatic theory of Truth and Objectivity (Haack 1998; Misak 2013; Rescher 2007) and those who following after James, most prominently Rorty (1982, 1999), consider such a project moot. Bacon (2012) summarizes Rorty's take on the role of truth indicating that "Rorty does not abandon the concept of truth. It is not a goal of inquiry because it is impossible for us to know that we have reached it, yet he insists upon the cautionary use of truth in order to contrast it with justification." Rorty argues simply that "*truth* is just the property that all true statements share" (Rorty 1982), of which little of interest can be said. Nevertheless, despite these differences, they all share a rejection of the idea of a neutral and ahistorical foundation of knowledge.

As Brandom (2003) puts it, we are all engaged in *the game of giving and asking for reasons*, a point that can be traced back to Sellars's (1956) rejection of *the myth of the given*:

> The essential point is that in characterizing an episode or a state as that of *knowing*, we are not giving an empirical description of that episode or state; we are placing it in the logical space of reasons, of justifying and being able to justify what one says. (p. 298–299)

1.2.4 Abandoning Representationalism

Another idea worth highlighting in the pragmatic tradition is the abandonment of representationalist theories, which are, in the words of Bernstein (2010), "theories that presuppose that the mind has impressions or ideas that represent objects that are 'outside of the mind' " (p. 140). Representational theories promote what Dewey (1929/1960) referred to as *the spectator theory of knowledge*; according to this theory, we human beings are observers of our environment, where we endeavor to collect information in order to develop even more exact descriptions of nature. This focus on the accuracy of the representation has been challenged by pragmatists, by proposing that we stop understanding theories and language as means for the accurate portrayal of nature, and start considering them in their role as instruments for manipulating nature (James 1907/1995). In the words of Rorty (1999):

> Pragmatists insist on nonocular, nonrepresentational ways of describing sensory perception, thought and language, because they would like to break down the distinction between knowing things and using them. (p. 50)

The breakdown of the distinction between knowing and using that Rorty describes invites us to reconsider the criteria that we rely upon for judging the quality of our theories. In particular, it prompts us to abandon the idea that theories should be evaluated in terms of similarity to nature.[5]

Pragmatist philosophers are not the only ones who advocate the move away from representationalism, and proponents of an alternative way of conceiving knowledge can also be found in cognitive sciences (Hutchins 2000; Núñez & Freeman 1999; Shanon 1993; Varela et al. 1991). An interesting example of a nonrepresentational perspective in cognitive psychology can be found in the work of Eleanor Rosch and her theories on concepts and categorization (Rosch 1978, 1999; Rosch & Lloyd 1978). As Margolis and Laurence (2014) indicate, it is widely accepted that concepts "are crucial to such psychological processes as categorization, inference, memory, learning, and decision-making"; however, the specifics of what concepts are, how they come to be formed, and how they fulfill their role in thought has become a controversial matter since the second half of the twentieth century (Laurence & Margolis 1999). Before the 1950s the perspective that predominated in the western tradition since Plato (see *Euthyphro*) was the *classical theory of concepts* or the *definition view*, according to which a conceptual category was a logical set clearly defined by a list of necessary and sufficient conditions (Margolis & Laurence 2014). As Rosch indicates, a corollary of this perspective is that "all instances possessing the criteria attributes have a full and equal degree of membership" (Rosch & Mervis 1975, p. 574). This classical/definitional perspective promotes thinking about concepts as representations of the outside world in the spirit of the spectator theory of knowledge. In her work, Rosch has proposed the *graded structure/prototype view*, a model in which:

> All categories show gradients of membership; that is, subjects easily, rapidly, and meaningfully rate how well a particular item fits their idea or image of the category to which the item belongs. Such judgments are the hallmark of the graded structure/prototype view (Rosch 1999, p. 66)

---

[5]From the pragmatic perspective I am proposing, your goals can imply empirical validation criteria, without having to make reference to a metaphysical reality. I can say, "look, historically the use of a given statistical fit index has been shown an effective way of selecting among models in this area", or alternatively argue that, "the field of statistics, which has been shown to be extremely useful in a number of disciplines in the past, suggests this criterion for judging a model". These are two potential rationales for using empirical validation (there may be many others), without appeals to "reality."

Rosch is a cognitive psychologist, not a pragmatic philosopher, but just as with Wittgenstein, I think that her work displays a distinct pragmatic affinity. Accordingly, I will use her theory of graded structure and prototypes as an additional instrument in my toolbox when outlining a pragmatic perspective on measurement.

1.2.5 Theories as Tools

The next question that we need to address is how would we proceed if we abandon the spectator theory of knowledge and we stop using similarity to reality as our criteria for evaluating our theories. How can we assess the quality of our knowledge? According to Dewey (1920/2004), there is a clear alternative:

> As in the case of all tools, [theories'] value resides not in themselves but in their capacity to work shown in the consequences of their use. (p. 83)

To put this in idea in concrete terms, let us think of a specific tool; say, a hammer. Do you decide that a hammer is good because of its resemblance to a "true" hammer? Probably not. Most likely, you will judge the quality of a hammer in terms of its capacity for assisting you in the completion of a task, such as driving in a nail while assembling a shelf. Pragmatism emphasizes the idea that we can consider our theories in the same light, and that instead of focusing on how closely they resemble nature, we are better off by asking ourselves how useful they are to the accomplishment of our goals. From this perspective, theories and language in general are considered to be "adaptation[s] to the environment, a set of tools for dealing with the causal pressures exerted by the environment, rather than a way of mirroring it" (Tartaglia 2007, p. 214).

In sum, pragmatism suggests us to evaluate our theories in terms of how they can help us cope with nature, as opposed to how accurate they are in representing it.

1.2.5.1 Pragmatism Recapped

This set of central ideas covered in the previous section, including the primacy of practice, fallibilism, anti-skepticism, the historical and social nature of knowledge, the anti-representational stance, and the conceptualization of our theories as tools, are nicely summarized by Menand (2001) in his book *The Metaphysical Club: A Story of Ideas in America*. In it, Menand discusses what he sees as the commonalities between the perspectives of James, Peirce, Dewey and Oliver Wendell Holmes, and in doing so he captures what I think is the gist of the pragmatic agenda by stating that:

> We can say that what these four thinkers had in common was not a group of ideas, but a single idea—an idea about ideas. They all believed that ideas are not 'out there' waiting to be discovered, but are tools—like

> forks and knives and microchips—that people devise to cope with the world in which they find themselves. They believed that ideas are produced not by individuals, but by groups of individuals—that ideas are social. They believed that ideas do not develop according to some inner logic of their own, but are entirely dependent, like germs, on their human carriers and the environment. And they believed that since ideas are provisional responses to particular and unreproducible circumstances, their survival depends not on their immutability but on their adaptability. (p. xi)

Having clarified how I am understanding pragmatism and how it impacts the way in which we understand knowledge, the next issue that must be addressed is how these ideas can help us rethink the concept of measurement in the social sciences. However, before tackling that issue it is necessary for us to briefly recap how measurement has been understood in the past decades, and that is the focus of the next chapter.

Chapter 2
What Is Measurement?

There are indeed myriads of definitions of measurement that have been proposed, influenced by the multiple areas in which the idea of measurement has been brought to bear. For a glimpse of the current widespread use of the concept of measurement we can look to the variety of areas of application of metrology, defined by the International Bureau of Weights and Measures as "the science of measurement, embracing both experimental and theoretical determinations at any level of uncertainty in any field of science and technology," which include manufacture of goods, international trade, satellite navigation, diagnosis in health related fields, and commerce (Bureau International des Poids et Mesures 2014). A similarly broad scope is represented in the twenty-four technical committees of the International Measurement Confederation, which include areas such as the measurement of force, mass, and torque (TC3), measurements in biology and medicine (TC13), and the measurement of human functions (TC18), the last one encompassing the "measurement, analysis and modeling of human functions, movement, perception and cognition" (International Measurement Confederation 2014). Interest in measurement goes beyond the physical sciences, playing a prominent role in economics (Boumans 2007; Spengler 1961), and education (Brennan 2006; Lindquist & Thorndike 1951), as well as sociology and psychology (Boring 1961; Duncan 1984; Lazarsfeld 1961), leading to the formation of organizations such as the Psychometric Society concerned with "the advancement of quantitative measurement practices in psychology, education and the social sciences" (Psychometric Society 2021).

Historically, few scholars in mathematics, physics, philosophy, and psychology have striven to present a unified definition of measurement. Some, like Michell (1997b), have turned to the history of the concept in the physical sciences to "properly define" what "scientific measurement" is. Others, like Berka (1983), for instance, have embraced the multiplicity of applications and have sought to distill the *essence* of measurement through the examination across context of applications:

D. Torres Irribarra, *A Pragmatic Perspective of Measurement*, SpringerBriefs in Psychology, https://doi.org/10.1007/978-3-030-74025-2_2

> It is much more important for the theory of measurement if we expound what can be meaningfully said about measurement from various standpoints: if we state what are the general and specific characteristics helping us to grasp the core of the method, what its role is in the process of scientific knowledge, under what conditions measurement can be legitimately applied, *and what indeed measurement is objectively* [emphasis added]. (p. 14)

Regardless of their strategy, the motivations for establishing (or discovering) *what measurement is* include attempts to identify solid foundations for the methods of science, to establish a demarcation criterion for what could and could not be measured, and to establish an encompassing definition that would facilitate communication across diverse knowledge domains.

Throughout history, the technical understanding of measurement has been influenced by key philosophical perspectives such as the "classical view" of measurement (Michell 2005), operationalism (Bridgman 1927), the representational theory of measurement (Krantz et al. 1971/2007; Pfanzagl 1968), as well as more methodological perspectives arising from the practice of researchers in the social sciences, such as latent variable perspective (Lazarsfeld & Henry 1968; Lord & Novick 1968; Rasch 1960/1980), and physical sciences and engineering, represented by metrology. The next sections present a brief overview of these influential strands but should not be in any way construed as an exhaustive review of the myriad of perspectives that have been proposed about the concept of measurement.

2.1 Classical Theory of Measurement

The Classical Theory of Measurement (CTM)[1] holds, generally speaking, that objects in reality have properties and that some of those properties are quantities. Measurement is seen as an activity concerned with the discovery and study of those quantitative properties.

Joel Michell (1997b; 1999; 2005), one of the strongest proponents of the return to the definitions of measurement laid out in the CTM, relies heavily on meticulous historical analysis of the concept of measurement and its origins in order to establish clear demarcation criteria regarding the correct way to practice measurement.

In his treatment of the CTM, Michell (2005) is explicitly committed to realism, which he defines in terms of commitment to a theory of truth that specifies "that a proposition is true if and only if things are as proposed" (p. 286). About this philosophical foundation, Michell states:

[1] Not to be confused with the Classical Test Theory in psychometrics (Lord & Novick 1968), despite some overlap in terminology.

> This literal concept of truth commits us to the existence of things... existing in time and space, independently of observation. The conviction that there is an objective, spatiotemporally structured world is *metaphysical realism* and the implication that things are logically independent of observation is *epistemological realism*. (p. 286)

From this perspective, Michell adopts a set of distinctions that go back to Aristotle's philosophical realism, chief among them the difference between *quantity* and *quality* as two of the fundamental categories that describe all that exist. Aristotle writes that "it is the distinctive mark of quantity that it can be called equal and unequal" (p. 17, trans. 2001) and "the fact that likeness and unlikeness can be predicated with reference to quality only, gives to that category its distinctive feature" (p. 27, trans. 2001). Aristotle further differentiates between two kinds of quantities, *multitudes* or *pluralities* which are discrete quantities,[2] and *magnitudes* which are continuous quantities, stating that "a quantum is a plurality if it is numerable, a magnitude if it is measurable" (p. 27, trans. 2001).

In the context of these classical distinctions, Michell (1990, 2005) traces the origin of CTM back to Book V of Euclid's *Elements* (trans. 1956). The first three definitions in Book V (p. 113–14) where a measure is defined as a ratio of one magnitude to another are:

1. A magnitude is a *part* of a magnitude, the less of the greater, when it measures the greater.
2. The greater is a *multiple* of the less when it is measured by the less.
3. A *ratio* is a sort of relation in respect of size between two magnitudes of the same kind.

The foundations of the CTM laid by Euclid in Book V and Book VII of the *Elements* were (much) latter fully axiomatized at beginning of the twentieth century by Otto Hölder (Michell & Ernst 1996, 1997),[3] and one year later an alternative axiomatization was proposed by Huntington (1902). Rooted in this treatment of magnitude, ratio and measure by Euclid and the axiomatization by Hölder, Michell (1997b) defines measurement as "the numerical estimation of the ratio of a magnitude of a quantitative attribute to a unit of the same attribute" (p. 383), going on to call the task of identifying whether a property of interest is or not a quantity the *scientific task* of measurement, as opposed to the *instrumental task* which focuses on the practicalities of conducting measurements.

The CTM establishes then a clear demarcation criterion for what constitutes measurement, which, according to Michell (1997b; 1999; 2005) had historically

---

[2] According to Michell (2011) the analysis of multitudes through frequencies is indeed quantitative, but not measurement: "Counting is a quantitative method, but not measurement (although it may be involved in processes of measurement)..." (p. 255). Footnote 1 (page 46) briefly touches on how is counting considered under the pragmatic perspective in this book.

[3] Hölder's original work was published in 1901 but was not translated into English until the late 1990s by Joel Michell and Catherine Ernst.

characterized measurement in the physical sciences by virtue of the discovery of quantities and the development of the appropriate instrumentation to determine their ratios.

According to Michell (2012b), all attributes can be classified into one of these three "structural possibilities":

> (1) *classificatory attributes* (with heterogeneous differences between categories);
> (2) *heterogeneous orders* (with heterogeneous differences between degrees); and
> (3) *quantitative attributes* (with thoroughly homogeneous differences between magnitudes). (p. 1)

Under CTM, the existence of quantity is the *sine qua non* condition of measurement. If the properties under study are not in themselves quantitative (i.e., if the answer to the *scientific task of measurement* is that they are classificatory or heterogeneous orders), there is no amount of work on the instrumental side that could ever justify the use of the word "measurement" in the study of such a property. It follows that if the true nature of a psychological property is qualitative, or ordinal for that matter, measurement of such a property is by definition impossible (Fig. 2.1).

The concept of measurement, Michell (1997b; 1999; 2005) claims, was then co-opted by the emergent discipline of psychology in the second half of the nineteenth century, and replaced by alternative, false definitions of measurement, that exempted psychology from seriously considering and conducting the scientific task of measurement, and casting doubt about the adequacy of any development on the instrumental task:

> *There is no evidence that the attributes that psychometricians aspire to measure (such as abilities, attitudes and personality traits) are quantitative.* Mainstream psychologists presumed that they are and that psychometric tests are suitable to measure them. All the evidence is that these attributes

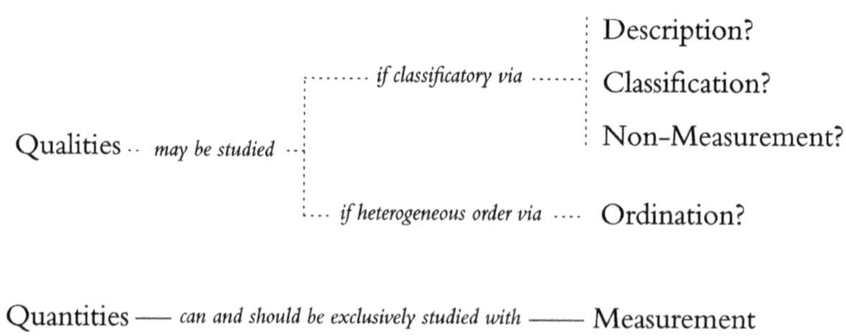

Fig. 2.1 Measurement and attributes in the classical theory of measurement

> are merely ordinal, and while psychologists are free to speculate about whether they might be quantitative, the fact is that, after a century, such speculations remain empty. (Michell 2011, p. 245)

Of course, the position that psychology, and potentially other social sciences, cannot engage in measurement because the attributes that are purported to be measured are not actually quantitative has a long history and is known as *the quantity objection* (Boring 1921):

> Introspection, the objection runs, does not show that a sensation of great magnitude ever contains other sensations of lesser magnitude in the way that a heavy weight may [supposedly] be made up of a number of smaller weights. "Our feeling of pink", said James, "is surely not a portion of our feeling of scarlet; nor does the light of an electric arc seem to contain that of a tallow-candle in itself." "This sensation of 'gray'," remarked Külpe, "is not two or three of that other sensation of 'gray' " (p. 453).

According to this objection, psychological properties are qualitative or in some cases ordinal, and therefore not subject to measurement; as Johnson (1936), a psychologist who adhered to this perspective asserts: "There are questions concerning human traits which are interesting; they may be important; they may be answerable; but they probably will remain unanswered as long as they are attacked by attempts to measure what is *intrinsically non-measurable* [emphasis added]" (p. 351).

However, all these criticisms to the core idea that psychological properties could be measured caused little impact and were ignored by a large majority of practitioners and researchers throughout the last century and a half of psychology (Cliff 1992; Hornstein 1988; Michell 1999).

2.2 Operationalism

Operationalism (Bridgman 1927) is perhaps the philosophical and methodological approach that presents the starkest contrast to the CTM. Developed originally by physicist P.W. Bridgman, this approach originated as his attempt to avoid the theoretical problems in physics that had been brought to light with the introduction of Einstein's theory of special relativity, of which Bridgman (1927) states:

> It was a great shock to discover that classical concepts, accepted unquestioningly, were inadequate to meet the actual situation, and the shock of this discovery has resulted in a critical attitude toward our whole conceptual structure which must at least in part be permanent. (p. 1)

Bridgman's efforts on this issue were focused on the elimination of ambiguity and confusion of concepts in physics due to the ever-present risk of extrapolation beyond areas directly examined by our experience. In his introduction of operationalism in *The Logic of Modern Science* (1927), he illustrates these issues by discussing the case of length, which he considers to be defined by the operations used to measure it.[4] To achieve his goal, Bridgman introduced the doctrine of *operational analysis*, according to which "we mean by any concept nothing more than a set of operations; the concept is synonymous with the corresponding set of operations" (Bridgman 1927, p. 5).

In philosophy of science, operationalism has been extensively criticized on a range of issues, ranging from challenges of attempting to equate the meaning of a theoretical term to a set of operations to more basic issues such as the lack of clarity of what should count as an operation (Chang 2009). However, for the purpose of this book, the most glaring issue with a strict operationalist perspective is the inability to coherently formulate the idea of multiple measures of the same attribute (Markus & Borsboom 2013), leading us to conclude that length, as measured by a ruler in centimeters, is an entirely different concept from length as measured in terms of parsecs by a telescope. This position and its consequences for measurement were explicitly advocated by Dingle (1950) in his paper *A Theory of Measurement*, where he stated:

> We must return to simplicity and describe what we do as faithfully as possible, without introducing conceptions which have outlived their usefulness. I therefore suggest the following definition: *A measurement is any precisely specified operation that yields a number.*

To be fair, both Bridgman (1927) and Dingle (1950) addressed the possibility of equating different sets of operations or attributes when their results could be compared, but considered this as a matter of practical convenience. Bridgman in particular still cautioned against assuming that such an equating procedure would amount to conceptual identity, an especially tempting possibility once we have summarized the treatment of a nanometer and a parsec as the same variable in a simple equation:

> The equations of motion make no distinction between the motion of a star into our galaxy from external space, and the motion of an electron about the nucleus, although physically the meaning in terms of operations of the quantities in the equations is entirely different in the two cases.... What we would like is some development of mathematics by which the equations could be made to cease to have meaning outside the range of numerical magnitude in which the physical concepts themselves have meaning. (Bridgman 1927, p. 63)

[4]"The concept of length is therefore fixed when the operations by which length is measured are fixed: that is, the concept of length involves as much as and nothing more than the set of operations by which length is determined" (Bridgman 1927, p. 5).

Measurement ——— *defines and can be used for studying* ——— Attributes

Fig. 2.2 Measurement and attributes in operationalism

Despite the problems that operationalism encountered as a philosophical doctrine, it was warmly adopted, and adapted, within psychology (Grace 2001; Green 1992). The influence of operationalism is still felt today through the idea of an *operational definition* of which Koch (1992) has acerbically remarked:

> The notion, as it now functions in psychology, is part of an empyrean of jargon that instructors draw upon in order to give students the illusion that they are studying a *science*. (p. 262)

As we have discussed, a strict operationalist approach eliminates the separation between defining a concept and measuring it, by making the former synonymous with the latter, and in principle raises the possibility of measuring any property, regardless of its structure (Fig. 2.2).

Although *prima facie* this may seem an invitation for an *anything goes* approach to measurement (and theory-building for that matter), it is important to remember that Bridgman, a renowned and Nobel winning physicist, was formulating his doctrine within the nomological network of physics and their shared practices. As Koch (1992) indicates, Bridgman presented his theory in this context as a way to help clarify concepts that already were part of the theoretical repertoire of physics, not as a way to create new concepts by defining them in an operational manner. Moreover, in *The Logic of Modern Science* (1927) Bridgman presents his arguments from a conception of measurement rooted in the tradition of physical measurement based on empirical operations. Alas, when operationalism was introduced to psychology, it would jettison some of these background assumptions and would be paired with a radically different approach to measurement.

2.3 The Representational Theory of Measurement

A third major strand that has influenced measurement theory, and arguably the predominant theory at the moment (Michell 1993; Narens 2013), at least among philosophers of measurement in the social sciences, is the Representational Theory of Measurement (RTM). This approach can be traced back originally to the work of Russell on the relation of number and quantity (1897), where he argued the independence of the notion of *number* from the notion of *quantity*, as opposed to the traditional view where numbers were based on quantity. In his review of Russell's 1903 critique to the traditional account of the number-quantity relation, Joel Michell (1997a) summarizes the central departure in the following way:

> The fundamental issue is whether or not ratios of magnitudes should be regarded as *instances* (Armstrong 1987) of real numbers. If they are understood in this way then the logic of the application of arithmetic to reality is that of *instantiation* rather than that of *representation*. (p. 270)

Russell (1903), based on this divorce between the concept of number and quantity, went on to state that "measurement of magnitudes is, in its most general sense, any method by which a unique and reciprocal correspondence is established between all or some of the magnitudes of a kind and all or some of the numbers, integral, rational, or real, as the case may be" (p. 176), laying the groundwork for the representational perspective that would be later popularized by the physicist Norman Campbell (1920), and that achieved its maturity with the work of Pfanzagl (1968) and the publication of the *Foundations of Measurement* volume by Krantz et al. (1971/2007).[5]

In contrast to the CTM, which is centered around the idea of estimating ratios of magnitudes, the RTM focuses on the "correlation with numbers of entities which are not numbers" (Nagel 1931, p. 313). This shift implies, in the words of Michell (1993), that "[the] numbers used in measurement are contributed to the measurement situation, rather than discovered within it" (p. 189). In practical terms, one of the main consequences of the decoupling of ratio estimation from measurement in the RTM was the "liberalization" of the concept of measurement to include ordering and classification, as was advocated in the version of the RTM developed by Stevens (1946).

2.3.1 Campbell: Between the Classical and Representational Theories

Campbell (1920) dedicated the second part of his book *Physics: The Elements* to the topic of measurement, beginning with the following definition: "Measurement is the assignment of numerals to represent properties" (p. 267).[6]In his theory of measurement, Campbell indicates that although an object may possess many attributes or qualities, not all of them can be measured. Campbell proposed that what made a property or quality measurable was our ability to relate that property to numbers in a very specific manner, namely, by empirically fulfilling relations of *order and additivity*.

[5]See Michell (1999) for an overview of the theoretical origins of the RTM and its departure from the classical conception of measurement in the work of Russell, Campbell, and Nagel.

[6]Berka (1983) points out that this is not Campbell's only definition throughout his work, characterizing it also as "the process of assigning numbers to represent qualities" (Campbell 1920, p. 267), "the assignment of numerals to represent properties according to scientific laws" (Campbell 1928, p. 1), and "the assignment of numerals to things so as to represent facts or conventions about them" (Campbell 1940, p. 340).

Campbell emphasized that an empirical process of concatenation was necessary in order to test experimentally whether the property conformed to the mathematical laws of order and addition. Based on this empirical criterion, he declared that "the difference between properties that are and those that are not capable of satisfactory addition is roughly that between quantities and qualities" (p. 267).

On this basis, Campbell then drew the distinction between *fundamental measurement* and *derived measurement*. Fundamental measurement applied to properties for which an empirical concatenation operation was available, with length, mass, and volume as examples. Derived measurement encompassed properties that lacked an empirical concatenation operation, but could be measured via other fundamentally measured properties. Density, for example, can be measured through mass and volume.

The focus on the need for empirical concatenation operations made Campbell's theory ideally suited to the work of physicists, but presented a serious challenge for social science disciplines such as psychology.

Campbell's theory can be considered a mixture between the CTM and RTM (Michell 1993, 1999), which on the one hand embraced classical intuitions such as the idea that only quantities could be subject to measurement, while on the other adopting the idea of measurement as correlation between empirical properties and a numerical system. It was on this aspect of the theory that some psychologists would rely to answer the challenge presented by Campbell's theory. On this unwitting outcome of Campbell's work Berka (1983) indicates:

> Although Campbell's monograph was programmatically opposed to any further extension of measurement, it nevertheless became the foundation of a general theory of measurement and the stimulation for its advancement of theoretical and methodological conceptions outside physics. (p. 13)

2.3.2 Stevens: Between the Representational and Operationalist Theories

S.S. Stevens' theory of measurement was developed as a direct answer to Campbell and his influential theory of fundamental and derived measurement. Stevens' response was presented as a challenge to the conclusions presented by a committee of the British Association for the Advancement of Science (BAAS), which had been tasked in 1932 with answering the question of whether sensations could be measured, a task that was conducted under the influential definitions of measurement proposed by Campbell, which demanded the existence of empirical concatenation operations.

In other words, the BAAS committee had been asked to judge whether measurement was possible in psychophysics. This judgment was conducted under Campbell's perspective on measurement, which was tailored after the physical sciences.

After working for the better part of a decade, the BAAS committee reported its results, which were described in the journal *Nature* as follows:

> It now seems that agreement is impossible. This is scarcely surprising when there is disagreement as to the meaning of "measurement". If it is postulated that this term must be limited to its applicability in physics, then this would rule out the use of the word in relation to much psychological work. Two extreme views hold the field, and a close examination of these views by a member who holds an intermediate view leads to the conclusion that they cannot be reconciled. (Nature Publishing Group 1939, p. 973)

In his 1946 paper *On the Theory of Scales of Measurement*, Stevens directly challenged the idea that the definition of measurement depended on the existence of empirical concatenation, indicating that "perhaps agreement can better be achieved if we recognize that measurement exists in a variety of forms and that scales of measurement fall into certain definite classes" (p. 677). Stevens went on to present this "variety of forms" by fully embracing the representational spirit of Campbell's definition while jettisoning its connection to the physical sciences, stating what by now has become a commonplace definition of measurement in psychology:

> We may say that measurement, in the broadest sense, is defined as the assignments of numerals to objects or events according to rules (p. 677).

While keeping the representational notion of the assignment of numerals to objects or events, Stevens switched the focus from the *empirical testing of the mapping* between properties and numbers, Campbell's original emphasis, to *the rules of that govern the mapping*: "The problem as to what is and is not measurement then reduces to the simple question: What are the rules, if any, under which numerals are assigned?" (p. 680). This focus on the mathematical properties that the rules of assignment entailed is at the basis of his taxonomy of *scale types*: nominal, ordinal, interval, and ratio scales (Stevens 1946).[7]

Each one of these four types of scales was defined according to Stevens by the kind of mathematical group structure associated with it and the set of permissible statistics that the scale would support (Stevens 1946). Table 2.1 reproduces the table originally presented in Stevens (1946).

Stevens (1946) taxonomy includes forms of non-quantitative measurement (i.e., the nominal and ordinal scales), in addition to the interval and ratio quantitative scales, but he barely acknowledged this considerable expansion of the term mea-

[7]It is worth noting that in his 1946 paper, Stevens discusses and details basic empirical operations associated with each one of the scale types. However, his summary regarding the characterization of measurement focuses exclusively in the rules of assignment and ignores completely any empirical requirements.

Table 2.1 Scale types as presented in Stevens (1946)

Scale	Basic empirical operations	Mathematical group structure	Permissible statistics (invariantive)
Nominal	Determination of equality	*Permutation group* $x' = f(x)$ $f(x)$ means any one-to-one substitution	Number of cases
			Mode
			Contingency correlation
Ordinal	Determination of greater and less	*Isotonic group* $x' = f(x)$ $f(x)$ means any monotonic increasing function	Median
			Percentiles
Interval	Determination of equality of intervals or differences	*General linear group* $x' = ax + b$	Mean
			Standard deviation
			Rank-order correlation
			Product-moment correlation
Ratio	Determination of equality of ratios	*Similarity group* $x' = ax$	Coefficient of variation

surement beyond quantity. In Stevens' treatment of measurement, the concept of quantity is relegated to the background.[8]

While Campbell's definition retained the idea that measurement could only be conducted when dealing with certain properties and not others, and at least implicitly indicating that this difference was somehow dependent on a property of nature itself, Stevens' new definition severed this connection, focusing solely on the procedure used to generate the assignment, allowing measurement of any property as long as a mapping was established according to rules.

Accordingly, Campbell's clear distinction between what is measurable and what is not measurable, with the quantitative on the former side, and the qualitative and ordinal on the latter, was also disregarded, effectively declaring that any kind of property was potentially measurable under one of the different scale types if the researcher developed a rule-based procedure to deal with it (Fig. 2.3). In other words, measurement was achieved by the sheer fact of establishing a rule-governed measurement procedure. If this sounds familiar, it is because it echoes Bridgman's operationalist doctrine described in Sect. 2.2 (Michell 1990).

[8] Stevens (1946) states at the beginning of his discussion on interval scales (after discussing both nominal and ordinal scales) that "with the interval scale we come to a form that is "quantitative" in the ordinary sense of the word." This is one of the only three allusions to quantity in his paper, and the only one outside direct quotes to the BAAS report.

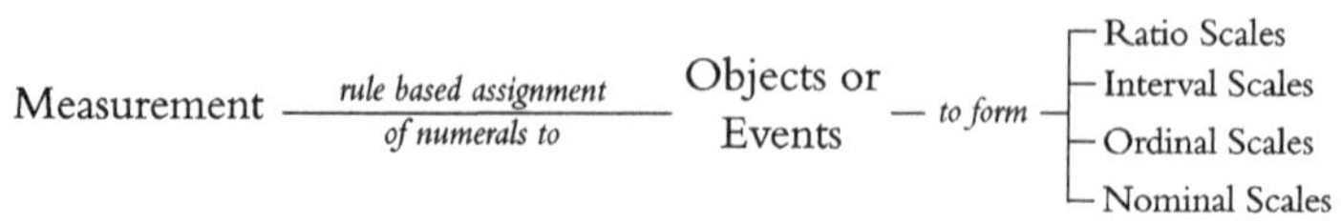

Fig. 2.3 Measurement and attributes in Steven's theory of measurement scales

It is worth pointing out, as Hand (2004) does, that even though Stevens' is usually cited (or criticized) for his 1946 definition of measurement "as the assignments of numerals to objects or events according to rules" (p. 677) and its sole focus on the rules of assignment, this was hardly the only aspect of the definition of measurement that he wrote about. In the very same 1946 article, Stevens highlights one of the definitions proposed by Campbell (1920):

> To the British Committee, then, we may venture to suggest by way of conclusion that the most liberal and useful definition of measurement is, as one of its members advised [i.e. Campbell], "the assignment of numerals to things so as to represent facts and conventions about them." (p. 680)

In contrast with the sole focus on the rules of assignment, this reference to Campbell's definition brings to bear the importance of "representing facts and conventions," a criterion that goes beyond the use of a non-random rule of assignment. Stevens would continue to emphasize the "representation of nature" stating, for instance, in 1951 that "the type of scale achieved when we deputize the numerals to serve as representatives for a state of affairs in nature depends upon the character of the basic empirical operations performed on nature" (p. 23). However, this disconnect between his more radically liberal statements about measurement and his more nuanced emphasis in the preservation of properties in nature through mathematical representations is unsurprising given Stevens' penchant for extremely memorable one-liners, such as "*in its broadest sense, measurement is the business of pinning numbers on things*" (Stevens 1958), a statement which he immediately followed with the much less remembered qualification:

> This process turns out to be a fruitful enterprise only because some degree of isomorphism obtains between the empirical relations among the properties of objects or events, on the one hand, and some of the properties of the number system on the other.

In any case, it was Stevens' emphasis on rules of assignment in his 1946 definition and its radical reinterpretation of the concept of measurement that would be remembered, encompassing many psychology methodologies under a new, much more liberal, theory of scales of measurement. However, it is important to note that Stevens' work presents a point of departure for two distinct traditions regarding the development and application of this new representational understanding of measurement, one focusing on his definition based on the rules of assignment, the other based on his stipulation on the need for isomorphism with empirical relations.

In the first tradition, Stevens' theory of scale types and its mixture between representational and operational measurement theory was adopted largely unchanged and was further popularized to the point of becoming a sort of received view of measurement in psychology and the social sciences in general; Duncan (1984, p. 125–126) stated on the ubiquity of this definition that "after all, most of what most of us know about measurement theory we learned from Stevens, if not directly then via some textbook author's secondary presentation." This strand embraced its operational nature (even though its philosophical background was not always explicitly acknowledged) (Green 1992, 2001). Torgerson (1958, p. 22) colorfully named this approach "measurement by fiat," but despite the skepticism that the name might invite, Torgerson did not dismiss this approach, stating that:

> It has led to a great many results of both practical and theoretical importance. For example, a major share of the results of the field of mental testing and of the quantitative assessment of personality traits has depended upon measurement by fiat. Measurement of morale, efficiency, drives, and emotion, as well as most sociological and economic indices, is largely measurement of this type (Torgerson 1958, p. 24).

However, not everyone was persuaded of the benefits of adopting this characterization of measurement. For example, it was later mocked by Wolins (1978, p. 1–2) as based simply in the argument that "we need interval measurement for certain types of statistical analysis, we don't really have it but we will pretend we do and everything will be all right." Stevens' theory of scale types would continue to exert a large influence, despite its critics in psychology (cf. Michell 1999), sociology (cf. Duncan 1984), and social statistics methodology (cf. Velleman & Wilkinson 1993) and continues to be the default definition of measurement even today in psychological methods textbooks (see, for instance, Elmes et al. 2012; Nestor & Schutt 2014).

In a separate, second tradition, the representational theory continued to evolve, taking Stevens' theory of scales as a starting point, and eventually leading to the formulation of axiomatic measurement theory (Krantz et al. 1971/2007; Luce et al. 1990/2007; Pfanzagl 1968). This more mature rendition of the representational approach would emerge as an alternative to the operationalist strand by embracing that "the more fruitful view is that the nature of a scale is defined by the relations exhibited among empirical variables" (Cliff 1992, p. 186), distancing itself from the operationalist commitments of the first strand.

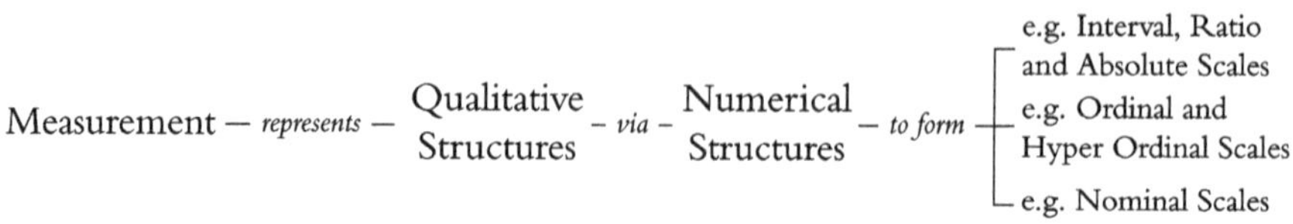

Fig. 2.4 Measurement and attributes in representational measurement theory

2.3.3 Axiomatic Measurement Theory

An extensive mathematical basis for representational measurement was developed in the form of Axiomatic or Abstract Measurement Theory (AMT; Krantz et al. 1971/2007; Luce & Tukey 1964; Scott & Suppes 1958; Suppes & Zinnes 1963).[9]

According to Narens and Luce (1986, p. 173), AMT holds at its core four conditions that are necessary for measurement: (1) an "ordered relational structure $\mathscr{X} = \langle X, \succsim, S_1, \ldots, S_n \rangle$, where $\succsim, S_1, \ldots, S_n$ are the *primitives* of the structure", (2) a set of axioms that describe the empirical structure (i.e., empirical laws), (3) a "a numerically based relational structure $\mathscr{R} = \langle R, \geq, R_1, \ldots, R_n \rangle$, where R is a subset of the real numbers and the R_i are relations and operations of comparable types to the corresponding empirical ones," and the fourth and last one:

> Which accomplishes measurement, is the proof of the existence of a structure preserving mapping from $\mathscr{X}$ into $\mathscr{R}$. We refer to $\mathscr{X}$ as the *empirical* or *qualitative structure*, $\mathscr{R}$ as the *representing structure*, and the structure-preserving mapping as a *homomorphism* or a *representation*. The collection of all homomorphisms into the same representing structure is referred to as a *scale*. (p. 173)

This framework sidestepped any debate about quantitative vs qualitative properties that concerned Campbell (and adherents to the CTM), by defining all measurement as based on the mapping of the *qualitative empirical structure* into a *representing numerical structure*. Instead of focusing on the "kinds of properties," the AMT followed Stevens' lead in using the concept of scales, now a formalized concept, developing it beyond Stevens (1946) original taxonomy (Fig. 2.4).

Under this new formalization of the concept of measurement, AMT subsumed the focus on physical variables of Campbell's fundamental measurement theory, replacing it with a more general redefinition idea of "fundamental measurement" based on numerical assignment, jettisoning Campbell's original requirement of an empirical concatenation operation as the sole foundation of measurement (Scott &

---

[9]A detailed overview of AMT is outside the scope of this book. Introductory texts to the basics of the theory can be found in Michell (1990), Narens and Luce (1986), and Narens (2013). An extensive treatment can be found in the three volumes of Foundations of Measurement (Krantz et al. 1971/2007; Luce et al. 1990/2007; Suppes et al. 1989/2007).

Suppes 1958; Suppes & Zinnes 1963). This reframed fundamental measurement as a part of a larger, psychology friendly, measurement theory (Narens & Luce 1986), of which Schönemann (1994) has commented:

> ... Campbell's version became a special case which the authors [Suppes and Zinnes] called "extensive measurement". This change in semantics enabled psychologists to charge Campbell with having been fundamentally mistaken: of course social scientists have fundamental measurement, they just do not have any extensive measurement.

A key achievement of this expansion of the concept of fundamental measurement was the development of Conjoint Measurement (Luce & Tukey 1964), which showed how to establish an interval scale based on the relations between a set of ordinal variables, without using an empirical concatenation operation (Narens & Luce 1986). In other words, AMT presented a mathematical foundation for using a quantitative scale solely on the basis of having identified a set of ordered variables and a specific set of relations. In principle, this was a colossal breakthrough, offering finally an answer to the challenge presented by Campbell and his theory to the possibility of measurement in psychology, and providing an overarching measurement framework across the physical and social sciences.

Nevertheless, the idea of psychological measurement that became commonplace was based on Stevens' original definition (i.e., measurement by fiat[10]), largely disregarding the advances made by AMT. In any case, the lack of impact of AMT on the practice of psychological measurement was memorably labeled "the revolution that never happened" by Cliff (1992), where he lamented that while in psychology "abstract measurement theory has to be regarded as one of its major intellectual achievements, viewed in terms of the power of thought that was required to achieve it and as a key pillar of the philosophy of science.... *it is clear that the influence of abstract measurement theory has been small* [emphasis added]" (p. 186). Although AMT has been adopted to conduct research on some areas of psychology (Narens & Luce 1993), its promise to serve as a foundation for measurement across the social sciences has largely been unfulfilled. However, it is worth noting that while advocates of the AMT tend to frame this issue as a problem of the larger psychological (and social science) community ignoring AMT's accomplishments, there is a case to be made that it was AMT that was developed while ignoring large parts of the measurements conducted in the social sciences and even some physical measurements (Adams 1979), and that the sparseness in its adoption is a product of this "strategy":

> One reason for the relative paucity of connections between measurement theory and substantive theory in psychology may arise from the fact that

[10]As an example of the extent to which AMT is considered by some scholars to be *the* definition of measurement, Dawes and Smith (1985) implicitly assume that anything other than AMT is effectively measurement by fiat, which they label as *non-representational measurement*.

> models for measurement have largely been developed independently as a body of abstract formal theory with empirical interpretations being left to a later stage. *The difficulty with this approach is that the later stage often fails to materialize.* [emphasis added] (Estes 1975, p. 273)

From this perspective, the lack of adoption of AMT is less surprising and can be attributed to some extent to the methodological and theoretical characteristics of the approach (cf. Schönemann 1994; Schwager 1991), such that:

> It is absurd to hold that these axioms state conditions which must be satisfied in order that measurement be possible, or that it be justified, since measurement clearly is possible and justified even though some of the measurement axioms are false. (Adams 1966, p. 131)

In trying to understand "Why did the revolution not occur?" (p. 188), Cliff (1992) entertains several hypotheses, both related to the larger research community and to the AMT itself, to account for the lack of influence of AMT in psychology (and the social science at large for that matter). These include the lack of the necessary level of mathematical knowledge among researchers, the lack of connections between the abstract mathematic treatment and the empirical challenges confronted by researchers, the lack of examples that attest to the "empirical power" of AMT (see also the 1994 paper by Schönemann for an elaboration on these criticisms). But perhaps more importantly, Cliff (1992) touches on what he calls "The Error Problem":

> Another kind of bridging element that has been lacking is ways to deal with failure to conform to the axioms. Measurement theory says that if certain conditions hold, then scales of a given kind are defined. If not, they are not. *But data always contradict one or the other axiom* [emphasis added]. What now? Error is always present in observation, yet how is it to be dealt with? How is one to deal with occasional failures of the cancellation axiom in conjoint measurement or transitivity in paired comparisons? The levels of variables are never infinitely fine, as is often required in the proofs. (p. 189)

And while Narens and Luce (1993) in general reject the charge that AMT has failed to produce practical applications that demonstrate its "empirical power," they acknowledge that, as opposed to statistics, "AMT focuses almost exclusively on structure, largely ignoring randomness" (p. 129), and that:

> Neither [AMT nor statistics] has any very clear idea about how to formulate the concept of randomness in a nonnumerical way. In particular, we simply do not know how to talk about randomness at a level involving only qualitative ordinal observations together with other qualitative relationships, such as combining two stimuli to form a third. (p. 129)

This issue had been previously raised in a more general manner by Adams (1979, p. 220): "A general difficulty with the current accounts is that they do not deal systematically with *error* and accuracy, which is in turn linked to the fact that they give no consideration to *variability* of objects over time, and the special role which *standards* play in measurement."

Although some efforts have been made to develop extensions to AMT that deal both with issues of accuracy (i.e., measurement with imperfect discrimination) through the use of semiorders (Adams 1965; Krantz 1967; Luce 1956) and accounts for error through random variability (Domingue 2014; Falmagne 1976, 1980; Perline et al. 1979), this remains an issue to this day. Interestingly, the problem of dealing with error is related to another factor that Cliff (1992) believes contributed to the lack of the influence of AMT, namely, the "distracting development" (p. 189) of covariance structure analysis and latent variable models in general, which do not see randomness as a problem, but are—for good or ill—dependent on it.

2.4 Latent Variable Modeling

Latent Variable Modeling can be considered more as a methodological tradition than an organized measurement theory. Nevertheless, its advocates and practitioners played an important role during the twentieth century in the popularization of statistical methods as a way of conducting measurement of psychological properties. The core intuition behind this tradition can be traced back to Charles Spearman, who discussed how the correlation between multiple observed variables was not only interesting in itself, but allowed for the possibility that "another—theoretically far more valuable—property may conceivably attach to one among the possible systems of values expressing the correlation; this is, that a measure might be afforded of the *hidden underlying cause of the variations*" (1904b, p.74). Spearman relied on this insight to introduce what became known as the *common factor model*, and he applied this approach to the measurement of intelligence (Spearman 1904a). With this novel development, Spearman contributed the basis for the concept of a latent variable to psychology's methodological armamentarium, while at the same time kickstarting the factorialist tradition of intelligence measurement.

At its core, the concept of latent variable modeling remains faithful to Spearman's initial use, namely, that we can reduce the complexity in a set of observed variables if we postulate a different, unobserved, underlying variable. This core idea behind latent variables has more recently been expressed under a general statistical framework as a "random variable whose realizations are hidden from us as opposed to manifest variables where these realizations are observed" (Skrondal & Rabe-Hesketh 2004).

Latent variables as a statistical tool can have multiple interpretations, but in psychology, and the social sciences more generally, they have been recurrently used as a measurement methodology that enabled researchers to study a wide variety of constructs (Skrondal & Rabe-Hesketh 2004). *Constructs* in this context is the name that is used to describe the attribute that the researcher is trying to measure (Messick 1989; Wilson 2005).

Although, it is important to point out that there is no official definition of measurement that has been endorsed, for instance, by major professional associations—as we will see is the case in Metrology—measurement in latent variable modeling is more often than not discussed in terms of Stevens' (1946) definition, and in some cases extending it. For instance, Lord and Novick (1968, p. 17) define measurement as "a procedure for the assignment of numbers (scores, measurements) to specified properties of experimental units in such a way to characterize and preserve specified relationships in the behavioral domain." Similar definitions, embracing the idea of measurement as *assignment* can be found, when measurement is defined, through the literature, for instance, Weitzenhoffer (1951), Guilford (1954, who attributes the definition to Campbell), Torgerson (1958), Crocker and Algina (1986), McDonald (1999), and de Ayala (2009). In this context, latent variable models are seen as a method of conducting this numerical assignment.

This approach to measurement has been described by van der Linden (1994) in the following manner:

> Modern measurement theory shows that we can go one step further and verify laws that explain observable data using only unmeasured variables. If these laws—or models, as modern measurement theory prefers to call them—are quantitative and empirically verified, then the unmeasured or latent variables have quantitative scales on which, as a byproduct, the positions of the objects are known. As the model contains only latent variables, measurement of them is not derived from other fundamentally measured variables—all variables are measured jointly, in relation to one another (p. 12)

Since its introduction in 1904, the study of latent variables has flourished, and expanded beyond the single, continuous latent trait methodology initially proposed by Spearman when modeling intelligence. Multiple frameworks have been proposed to account for the myriad of variations and areas of development (see Langeheine and Rost (1988), Heinen (1996), and Skrondal and Rabe-Hesketh (2004) for reviews of the extensive family of latent variable models). One important and relatively early framework, Latent Structure Analysis (Lazarsfeld & Henry 1968, henceforth LSA), included continuous (latent trait models), categorical (latent classes), and ordinal (ordered latent classes) variables, illustrating how this methodology could be applied to model attributes of different structures (Fig. 2.5).

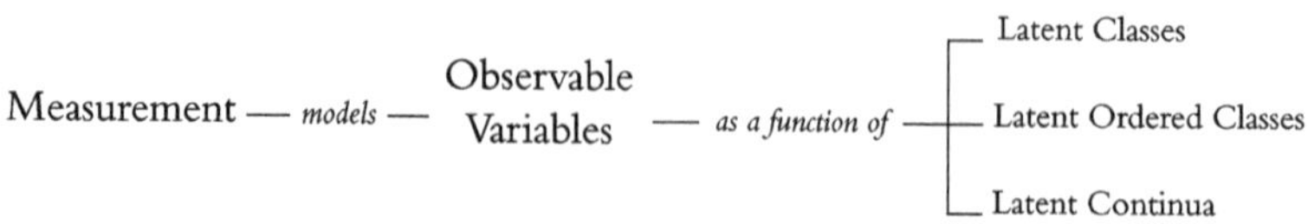

Fig. 2.5 Measurement and attributes in latent variable modeling

An example of the treatment of latent variable modeling as a measurement approach is presented by de Ayala (2009) where he indicates:

> The measurement process involve deciding whether our latent variable, anxiety, should be conceptualized as categorical, continuous, or both. In the categorical case we would classify individuals into qualitatively different latent groups so that, for example, one group may be interpreted as representing individuals with incapacitating anxiety and another group representing individuals without anxiety. In this conceptualization the persons differ from one another in *kind* on the latent variable. Typically, these latent categories are referred to as *latent classes*. Alternatively; anxiety could be conceptualized as continuous. From this perspective, individuals differ from one another in their *quantity* of the latent variable. Thus, we might label the ends of the latent continuum as. say, "high anxiety" and "low anxiety." (p. 2)

Many different structures of the latent variable can be hypothesized, and models have been proposed to deal with each one of these structures. For instance, see the five different possibilities presented in Fig. 2.6.

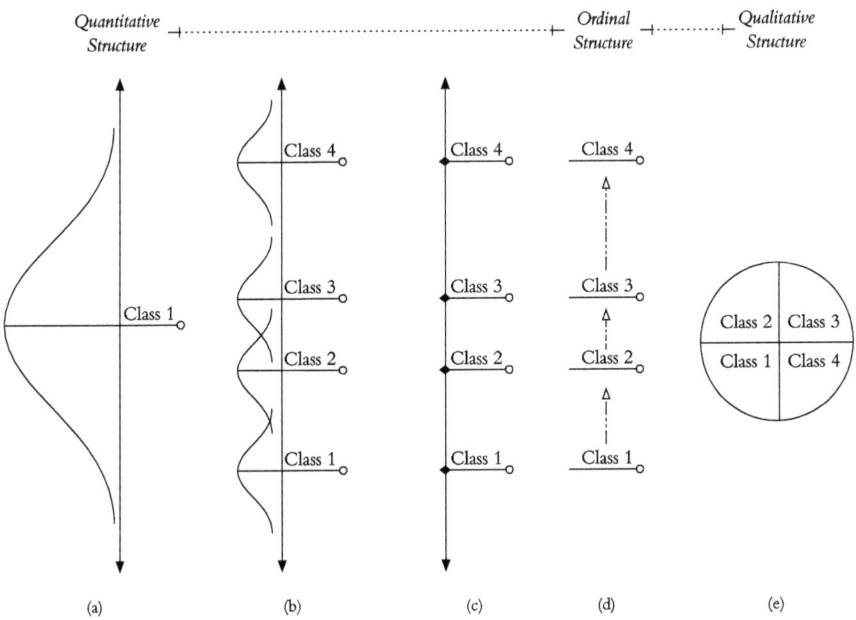

Fig. 2.6 Alternative models of a latent variable. (**a**) Continuous quantitative variable. (**b**) Located heterogeneous classes. (**c**) Located homogeneous classes. (**d**) Ordered classes. (**e**) Qualitative classes

The structure in pane (a) in Fig. 2.6 is perhaps the most popular way of conceptualizing variables in psychology and, accordingly, one with an extensive line of research in the area of item response modeling (Birnbaum 1968; Rasch 1960/1980). However, scholars in latent variable modeling have proposed models for dealing with the other kinds of structures (usually under the label of mixture models) presented in panes (b) to (e): heterogeneous located latent classes (Lubke & Muthen 2005; Muthen & Asparouhov 2006), homogeneous located latent classes (Formann 1995; Uebersax 1993), ordinal latent classes (Croon 1990, 1991, 2002; Van Onna 2004), and of course, latent class analysis (Hagenaars & McCutcheon 2002; Lazarsfeld & Henry 1968).

2.5 Metrology

As a discipline dedicated to measurement, metrology is not exclusively concerned with the theoretical foundations of measurement, but also with the practical aspects associated with maintaining the measurement infrastructure that supports 80% of global trade (Kaarls 2007). Achieving coordination at this scale is not a trivial matter and has prompted efforts of multiple international organizations concerned with measurement, including the International Bureau of Weights and Measures (BIPM) to establish the Joint Committee for Guides in Metrology.[11]This committee is responsible for the development and maintenance of two central reference documents: the *International Vocabulary of Metrology* (VIM for its acronym in French; Joint Committee for Guides in Metrology 2012) and the *Guide to the Expression of Uncertainty in Measurement* (GUM; Joint Committee for Guides in Metrology 2008).

The VIM states that its purpose is "to be a common reference for scientists and engineers—including physicists, chemists, medical scientists—as well as for both teachers and practitioners involved in planning or performing measurements, irrespective of the level of measurement uncertainty and irrespective of the field of application. It is also meant to be a reference for governmental and inter-governmental bodies, trade associations, accreditation bodies, regulators, and professional societies" (p. 1). To achieve this, the VIM presents a consensus perspective, that while acknowledging differences between the areas of application, assumes that "there is no fundamental difference in the basic principles of measurement." Since it was first published in 1984, the VIM is now in its third edition in an attempt to remain

[11]The member organizations are the International Bureau of Weights and Measures (BIPM), the International Electrotechnical Commission (IEC), the International Federation of Clinical Chemistry and Laboratory Medicine (IFCC), the International Organization for Standardization (ISO), the International Union of Pure and Applied Chemistry (IUPAC), the International Union of Pure and Applied Physics (IUPAP), the International Organization of Legal Metrology (OIML), and the International Laboratory Accreditation Cooperation (ILAC).

a living document that responds to new areas of application and developments in metrology (Mari 2014).

In its latest iteration, the VIM includes definitions of more than 140 concepts, which outline the basis for conducting measurements and communicating measurement results. A key concept that is defined is quantity, which is characterized as a "property of a phenomenon, body, or substance, where the property has a magnitude that can be expressed as a number and a reference," in opposition to nominal properties, which are "propert[ies] of a phenomenon, body, or substance, where the property has no magnitude." Up to this point, the VIM is consistent with the distinction between quantity and quality that was discussed in Sect. 2.1; however, the VIM departs from this separation with the inclusion of ordinal properties as a type of quantity. An ordinal quantity is defined as a "quantity, defined by a conventional measurement procedure, for which a total ordering relation can be established, according to magnitude, with other quantities of the same kind, but for which no algebraic operations among those quantities exist."

With these three kinds of properties in the background (quantities, ordinal quantities and nominal properties), the VIM defines measurement as the "process of experimentally obtaining one or more quantity values that can reasonably be attributed to a quantity" (p. 16) and accompanies this definition with three notes: (a) nominal properties cannot be measured (Fig. 2.7), (b) measurement involves comparing quantities or counting entities, and (c) "measurement presupposes a description of the quantity commensurate with the intended use of a measurement result, a measurement procedure, and a calibrated measuring system operating according to the specified measurement procedure, including the measurement conditions."

The definition in the VIM is interesting when compared with the previous perspectives, as it emphasizes the experimental aspects involved in measurement, and while the definition may appear vague when referring to "reasonable attribution," the third note explicitly discusses conceptual and practical aspects that must be involved in measurement.

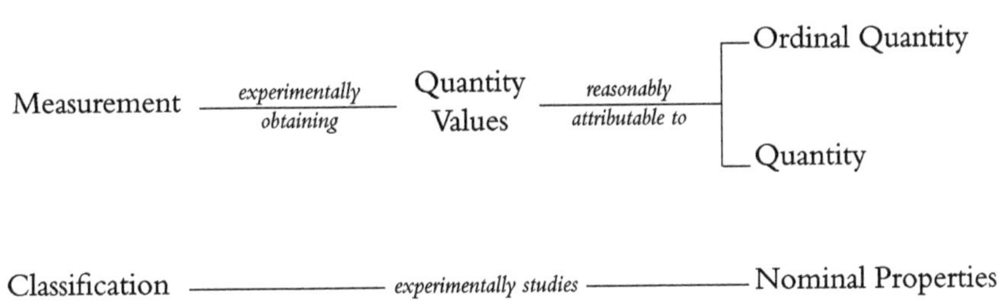

Fig. 2.7 Measurement and attributes in metrology according to the VIM

2.6 Defining Measurement?

The previous sections presented a brief review of multiple definitions of measurement associated with several theoretical approaches, each emphasizing different aspects and answering to the varied demands of different domains of application. Any one of these definitions could be used to draw a distinction between who is *truly* doing measurement, and who is only pretending to do so, and depending on our preference, could divide the field between those who are on the right side of the definition and those who should be forced to renounce the use of the word "measurement."

However, regardless of these efforts to define or prescribe what measurement is and how it should be practiced, researchers and practitioners in physics, chemistry, engineering, medicine, epidemiology, psychiatry, psychology, sociology, political science, philosophy, and economics are routinely attempting to conduct measurement as part of their work, each one conducts their work under different theoretical traditions, but presumably, all aim to achieve some of the "precision and objectivity" (Porter 1996, p. 23) associated with the concept of measurement. As Finkelstein (2003, p. 39) has remarked, "the requirements of those wider domains of knowledge and reasoning have led to the broadening of the concept of measurement, so as to encompass other forms of symbolic description." Considering the tensions between this increasing "broadening" of the definition of measurement and its tensions with narrower conceptualizations, the next chapters focus in discussing how an intuition from a pragmatic perspective can help us reconcile this alternative definition.

Chapter 3
Measurement: Prototypes and Resemblances

In light of the varied ways in which measurement is practiced, Mari (2013) indicates that, "since in the scientific and technical literature multiple, sometimes incompatible, definitions of 'measurement' can be found, identifying a single conceptual framework is a significant target for measurement science ..." (p. 2889). It is the search for this common conceptual framework that has prompted the development throughout history of different, and successively broader, characterizations of measurement in an effort to acknowledge new areas of application. The spirit of this search is nicely captured by Duncan (1984):

> And if theory of measurement, more broadly conceived than the theory of scale types, stops short of accounting for these measures which are among our main working tools, we must create a more comprehensive theory of social quantification. (p. 154)

It is worth noting that Duncan (1984) had serious reservations about Stevens' theory and considered, for instance, that his inclusion of nominal scales as a level of measurement was a mistake. Nevertheless, as the above quote indicates, his commitment was to the creation and adoption of a definition of measurement that accounted for *our main working tools*.

However, not all scholars subscribe to this program, generating tensions between those who favor more encompassing definitions of measurement by considering socio-historical factors versus those who favor a time-invariant conception of measurement, cautioning about potential redefinitions as the work of "uncritical scientist[s] in a particular area [who] could, for socio-historical reasons, come to misunderstand a concept such as measurement and use it in ways inconsistent with its wider theoretical commitments" (Michell 1999, p. 2).

D. Torres Irribarra, *A Pragmatic Perspective of Measurement*, SpringerBriefs in Psychology, https://doi.org/10.1007/978-3-030-74025-2_3

3.1 The Many Faces of Measurement

The contrast between these two "poles" has naturally prompted some scholars to look for a middle ground, a third way so to speak, as can be seen in Savage (1970) where he contrasts *the narrow view*, which has a stringent definition rooted in classical notions that had served well the old physical sciences since Aristotle, and *the broad view* of measurement, which attempts to adapt and extend both the concept and practice of measurement. This push for flexibility in the latter view has been associated with a drive to serve the needs of the fledgling new psychological science and satisfy the demands that society at large increasingly put on it (cf. Hornstein 1988; Michell 1999), and of course, the lack of success found in the straight imitation of the measurement techniques of the physical sciences. Berka (1983) echoes this dilemma, asking:

> In what extension should we then conceive of the concept of measurement? Under the influence of the extensions of measurements in the social sciences, two different levels of measurement are usually differentiated: the so-called *lower* level (classification, numbering, numeral designation and ordering) and the so-called *higher* level, which corresponds to the scope of measurement as it is understood in the context of physical measurement. These different levels are also terminologically fixed by virtue of the differentiation between qualitative and quantitative measurement, or between classical and liberalized theories of measurement. In the same sense, we shall speak for the time being about the *wider* and *narrower* comprehensions of measurement. (p. 33)

Considering both of the extreme positions unacceptable, Savage expresses the desire to find a characterization of measurement that "is as broad as it can be without doing undue violence to the ordinary meaning or to the technical meaning of the term 'measurement' " (p. 197).

However, if at some point the movement toward a broader definition was spearheaded solely by researchers and practitioners in psychology and the social sciences, this is no longer the case. An interesting example of this lies in the point of contention between the CTM and the more liberal definitions and relates to the possibility of measuring ordinal attributes. As indicated in Sect. 2.1, under the Aristotelian distinctions embraced by the classical conception of measurement, ordinal attributes are qualities, not quantities, and therefore cannot be measured, as measurement can only be performed when dealing with quantitative attributes (Johnson 1936; Michell 1997b, 1999, 2005, 2020). The representational measurement theory (Krantz et al. 1971/2007; Pfanzagl 1968; Stevens 1946) does not abide by the same restrictions, explicitly allowing the creation of ordinal measurement scales. Michell (2012a), perhaps the most prominent advocate in the last couple of decades for the classical, more stringent, perspective of measurement, considers that "merely ordinal attributes with impure differences of degree, [are] a feature logically incompatible with quantitative structure" (p. 255) and charges psychology and the social sciences with deluding themselves for attempting to measure such qualities. However, the acceptance of the possibility of ordinal measurement is in fact not restricted to psychology and the social sciences, but is part of the conceptual toolbox of modern metrology, where the concept of *ordinal quantity* is officially recognized in the International Vocabulary of Metrology (Joint Committee for Guides in Metrology 2012), effectively placing the International Bureau of Weights and Measures, home of the International System of Units, in disagreement with the classical definition of measurement.

The drive to separate classification, ordering, and quantification in the current context also seems to ignore the distinction between the assumptions that we have about the attribute that is being modeled and the methods used to investigate it. This difference is important in light of the current use of statistics to model attributes of interest that are not only quantitative but also ordered and qualitatively different. The confusion between the characterization of the methods and the hypothesized structure of the attribute of interest hinges on an important ambiguity in the meaning of "quantitative" and "quantity." We can see the conflation between the type of methods used to study an attribute of interest and the structure of said attribute in this quote by Michell (2012b):

> One of the defects of Stevens's well known classification of "scales of measurement" (Stevens 1946) is that in assimilating classifications ("nominal scales" in Stevens's terms) and orderings ("ordinal scales") into his concept of measurement, the conceptual difference between the *qualitative methods of classifying and ordering* and the *quantitative method of measurement* is obscured [emphasis added]. The simplest way to see this difference is to note the fact that in "nominal" and "ordinal scaling" the use of numerals is optional because all of the information contained in such "scales" can be expressed non-numerically. For example, the classes comprising a classification can be given non-numerical names and the categories constituting an ordering can be designated using terms from any ordered series, such as letters of the alphabet. (p. 6)

In this quote, we can see how Michell is bundling the type of methodology used to study the attribute with the model of scale type or structure of the attribute, rejecting *a priori* the possibility of using *quantitative* methods for classification and ordering as well as *qualitative* methods for measuring. I contend that the current use of latent variable models to study latent classes and ordered latent classes does in fact allow us to conduct the former, and as I will argue later in Chap. 5, the latter is an integral part of the process of studying "quantitative attributes."[1]

[1]It is important to clarify that I am in no way implying that we can fully examine qualities through quantitative methods nor quantities through qualitative methods. I am simply stating that the use of either methodology is in principle possible and can yield useful outcomes.

If we go back to what is considered one of the first definitions of a quantity, we will find that Euclid's definition is restricted to ratios of magnitudes (see Sect. 2.1). Later on, Hölder's axiomatization still considered quantity as ratios of magnitudes, but extended their application to intervals between points on a line (Hölder 1901; Michell and Ernst 1996, 1997). Similarly to Hölder, Stevens (1946) considered "quantitative" to apply to his interval and ratio scales. At the same time, latent variable modeling as a tradition is usually considered a "quantitative" methodology for its reliance on the likelihood of observing specific events through the use probability and statistics. On this regard, it is possible to see that the probabilities of observing specific events (and their typical odds and logit transformations) can serve as a basis for quantitative analysis of latent attributes of different structures.

In the use of a probabilistic statistical model, "quantitative" has a much broader scope than the definitions of quantitative by Euclid, Hölder or even Stevens (1946). Why? because within a framework such as LSA, those probabilistic statistical methods are not restricted to study attributes that are "quantitative" in Hölder's sense, and can be explicitly applied to study attributes that are hypothesized to be qualitative or ordinal and modeled through their effects observable variables. In other words, "quantitative methods" in that larger sense, when applied in a measurement context, do not presuppose that the latent variable is "quantitative" in the narrow sense.

In sum, the concept of measurement, and that of quantitative methods, is currently being used across the board in ways that do not necessarily conform to traditional (i.e., classical) definitions of measurement, pushing the boundaries of what constitutes "undue violence" to our technical understanding of it. Moreover, what constitutes a technical understanding of measurement, and the theoretical commitments that it entails will vary in different areas. In this context, disagreement on what is constitutive of measurement is bound to appear. For example, Mari (2013), in his review of the literature, finds definitions that focus on the structure of the measurement process, the results of the measurement process, the comparison to a unit of reference, and the requirement of the correspondence to numbers.

Pragmatism offers here the advantage of being flexible and fallibilist, encouraging us to abandon the fantasy of a timeless and perfect definition that attempts to establish decontextualized/definitive demarcation criteria for what is truly measurement.

3.2 Protypes and Resemblances

It is my view that the attempt to establish a single demarcation criterion does not do justice to the range of current well accepted practice. On the one hand, it is unclear that we can "put the genie back in the bottle" and return to a more restricted understanding of measurement in order to rein in what is now a broad "ordinary meaning" in favor of a stringent and idealized "technical meaning." On the other hand, it seems legitimate to be concerned about misunderstanding and possible misrepresentation if we acknowledge that we have different communities using measurement in different ways. Is there a way to acknowledge different practices and approaches as engaging in the overall endeavor of measurement, while at the same time acknowledging their differences? I think the answer is yes, and it involves recognizing that the search for a single definition of measurement is in a broader sense a problem of categorization, which is usually approached by attempting to provide a clear technical definition of the concept of measurement. Trying to characterize the meaning of a concept in this manner is consistent with what is called the *classical theory of concepts* as discussed in Sect. 1.2.4, and adopting Rosch's (1978; 1999) *prototype and graded structure account* might help in handling the multiplicity of definitions and approaches to measurement.

Laurence & Margolis (1999) present an example of how the classical approach characterizes a concept by using the example of the concept of *bachelor*:

> So BACHELOR might be composed of a set of representations such as IS NOT MARRIED, IS MALE, and IS AN ADULT (p. 9).

Based on such a definition, the classical theory predicts (a) that categorization should be a clear cut matter (i.e., you either fulfill or do not fulfill the set of necessary and sufficient conditions), (b) that all members of a category are equal members, and (c) that we should be able to specify these conditions for concepts that we use (Medin 1989).

However, empirical evidence contradicts these predictions, indicating that people encounter unclear and fuzzy cases (Laurence & Margolis 1999; Medin 1989). Similarly, it seems that within a given category some elements are indeed "more equal" than others. As Medin (1989) indicates when summarizing these findings, "people judge a robin to be a better example of bird than an ostrich is and can answer category membership questions more quickly for good examples than for poor examples" (p. 9).

A key feature of Rosch's account stems from its explicit recognition that for any given category, not every one of its members was considered to be equally representative of it; in her theory, she referred to the "best examples" of a category as *prototypes*. Many different factors can account for what makes a specific example prototypical of category, including elements varying from the frequency of the example to cultural and physiological factors (Rosch 1999). For instance, what counts as a prototype can vary from one context to another, such as in the case of animals: "while dog or cat might be given as prototypical pet animals, lion or elephant are more likely to be given as prototypical circus animals" (Rosch 1999, p. 67).

Finally, empirical results indicate that we are not as good at identifying the necessary and sufficient attributes required to define a category as the traditional view expected (Rosch & Mervis 1975). By contrast "attributes appeared to have a family resemblance (Wittgenstein, 1953), rather than a necessary and sufficient structure." (Rosch 1999, p. 67).

The notion of a relation of *family resemblance* between members of a category was famously illustrated by Wittgenstein (1953/2003) with the example of what counts as a "game":

> Consider for example the proceedings that we call "games". I mean board-games, card-games, ball-games, Olympic games, and so on. What is common to them all?—Don't say: "There must be something common, or they would not be called 'games'"—but look and see whether there is anything common to all. For if you look at them you will not see something that is common to all, but similarities, relationships, and a whole series of them at that. To repeat: don't think, but look!—Look for example at board-games, with their multifarious relationships. Now pass to card-games; here you find many correspondences with the first group, but many common features drop out, and others appear. When we pass next to ball-games, much that is common is retained, but much is lost.—Are they all 'amusing'? Compare chess with noughts and crosses. Or is there always winning and losing, or competition between players? Think of patience. In ball games there is winning and losing; but when a child throws his ball at the wall and catches it again, this feature has disappeared. Look at the parts played by skill and luck; and at the difference between skill in chess and skill in tennis. Think now of games like ring-a-ring-a-roses; here is the element of amusement, but how many other characteristic features have disappeared! And we can go through the many, many other groups of games in the same way; can see how similarities crop up and disappear. And the result of this examination is: we see a complicated network of similarities overlapping and criss-crossing: sometimes overall similarities, sometimes similarities of detail.
>
> I can think of no better expression to characterize these similarities than 'family resemblances'; for the various resemblances between members of a family: build, features, colour of eyes, gait, temperament, etc. etc. overlap and criss-cross in the same way.—And I shall say: 'games' form a family. (§66–67; p. 27e–28e)

This notion is markedly different from a traditional view of categorization, which demands that all members of a category share the same set of necessary and sufficient attributes. Rosch follows Wittgenstein in arguing that our concepts are extended "as in spinning a thread we twist fibre on fibre. And the strength of the thread does not reside in the fact that some one fibre runs through its whole length, but in the overlapping of many fibres" (Wittgenstein 1953/2003, p. 28e).

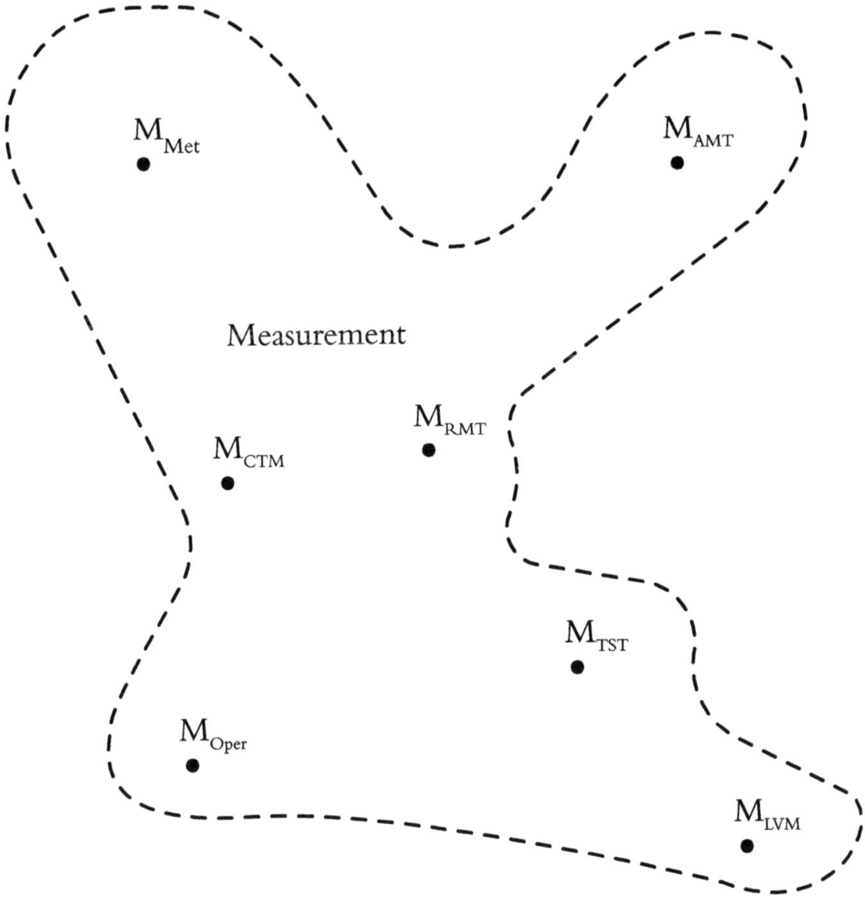

Fig. 3.1 Multiple prototypes of measurement

3.3 Prototypical Measurement Practices

I think that the framework provided by the prototype/graded structure research program, and Wittgenstein's notion of family resemblance, can help us organize and clarify the multiple relations and differences between alternative approaches to characterizing measurement.

From this perspective, it is possible to recognize the role of more traditional approaches to measurement as prototypical instances of measurement (e.g., determining the length of a table with a ruler), without restricting the concept to them. As mentioned above, this framework also recognizes that which prototype will be considered as representative of concept depends on the context, which can also help reconcile that "length and a ruler" can come to mind when talking casually about measurement, and "math knowledge and a quiz" when talking about teachers and classrooms or "literacy and PISA" when discussing educational policy.

To show how thinking about measurement definitions in this way can help, consider the diagram in Fig. 3.1. This diagram is meant to represent different measurement practices according to different communities within the larger, amoeba-shaped, scope of the practices that use the concept of, and purport to conduct, "measurement." Within this area, the diagram highlights seven points, each representing a prototypical measurement practice according to the theories reviewed earlier.

We can begin reviewing this diagram with one prototypical measurement practice, the classical theory of measurement, labeled M_{CTM} and located more or less at the left center, which historically constituted a most influential prototype of the notion of measurement. This prototype is surrounded by other measurement practices that have emerged as the use of the concept has changed and adapted to the needs and use cases of different communities of researchers or users, including in this case metrology M_{Met}, the representational measurement theory M_{RMT}, axiomatic measurement theory M_{AMT}, operationalism M_{Oper}, Stevens' typology of scale types M_{TST}, and latent variable modeling M_{LVM}.

As the meaning of measurement is expanded, some features are dropped and others preserved, maintaining perhaps only a family resemblance relation to each other. Faced with this situation, there are those who advocate a specific practice and say "this is the true definition of measurement," and thus can correctly point out that the other practices do not have the set of attributes that they deem necessary. Based on this issue, those who favor the practice of M_{CTM} as the prototype of measurement want everyone else to stop using the concept of measurement and refer to what they are doing as something else. This is a most stringent way that we could approach the definition of measurement and it seems to me an option that is unhelpful in promoting good practices across the whole amoeba-like area.

On the other extreme, there are those who claim that measurement is the entire amoeba-shaped area, and under that premise, claim that all practices are equal members, all benefiting from the credibility that emanates from the concept of measurement. On this end, instances of measurement under Dingle (1950)'s radical operationalism would have to be considered as equivalent to any other measurement conducted under axiomatic measurement theory, latent variable modeling, or metrological procedure. In other words, under the idea that measurement is an all-or-nothing proposition, everything we allow ourselves to consider as "measurement" becomes and equal member in the classification: a 22-year-old unmarried college student and the Pope are both bachelors after all. This is the most liberal way to approach to understanding measurement and it seems to me equally unreasonable.

A different issue may arise in between these extremes if some measurement practices under one prototype (e.g., M_{TST}) are being mistakenly identified by the public as practicing measurement according to a different prototype, (M_{Met}), either by miscommunication, or worse, by misrepresentation.

The account that I propose emphasizes the fact that these alternate measurement practices are indeed different in more ways than one, and while they all embrace the concept of measurement, it is unwarranted to simply assume that their different measurement practices will underwrite claims with the same precision. By acknowledging a more complex structure to the use of the concept of measurement we can abandon the all-or-nothing propositions that, on one extreme would prohibit uttering the word "measurement" outside the classical understanding,[2]and on the other would attempt to establish all measurement practices as equally precise and established.

The large amount of white inside the space amoeba-like area in the diagram also hints at another aspect of measurement practice that is worth highlighting, namely, that although we can identify a certain set of ideal prototypes under each approach (the black points in this case), most of the work on measurement occurs in the space between of these ideal types (not prototypical), but still within the realm of measurement. In other words, when scholars engage in discussions about measurement or when practitioners conduct measurements, they do so under the influence of multiple approaches. I would go as far as to argue that what is considered "measurement" for those who use the concept but do not study it directly is likely nothing more than the collection of practices of the prototypes that are closer to their area of application, which are usually adopted without explicit mention or allegiance to one or other of these prototypes.

[2]Or metrological if its practitioners suddenly start advocating for their right to the throne of the kingdom of measurement.

Chapter 4
A Pragmatic Perspective of Measurement

I have argued for the idea that the multiple measurement practices discussed earlier are related by a set of family resemblances to each other, where each measurement prototype highlights different aspects depending on its emphasis and context of application. Framing the myriad of definitions and theories as different prototypes, with shared family resemblances to each other, allows us to consider them in a complementary way instead of thinking of them as fully opposed, competing after the position of single, true definition.

I have also argued that because of this set of resemblances, attempting to define measurement with a single and clear cut definition might not be the best strategy if we are committed to developing a comprehensive understanding, and improvement, of measurement across different disciplines. This is not meant to dismiss the attempt to characterize measurement through definitions and theories, but to demand less of them. In particular, to stop expecting them to present an exhaustive characterization with clear cut limits, and think of them more as maps that allow us to highlight relevant elements of the practice of measurement under the varied demands that emerge in different areas of application.

In this context, I would like to present a Pragmatic Perspective of Measurement (PPM) to highlight what I see as some key commonalities that are shared by most of the measurement approaches previously discussed. By leveraging the emphasis of Pragmatism on the ideas presented in Sect. 1.1, I aim to present a characterization of measurement that highlights some of the family resemblances, without pretending to be exhaustive or prescriptive.

Pragmatism offers an interesting alternative to a core assumption shared by some of the major accounts of measurement, namely the classical and representational theories of measurement. Despite their differences, these theories assume that there is a true structure, either of the attribute or the qualitative empirical relations, that we are trying to recover or replicate. Accordingly, a measurement is good to the extent that it resembles this true structure and approximates true values. Pragmatism invites us to look for an alternative conception of measurement that eschews this copying

D. Torres Irribarra, *A Pragmatic Perspective of Measurement*, SpringerBriefs in Psychology, https://doi.org/10.1007/978-3-030-74025-2_4

metaphor, and with it, a set of theoretical and philosophical problems related to the definition and demarcation of measurement.

When thinking on how to characterize a domain of knowledge from a Pragmatic perspective, I find James' (1907/1995) example of a radical Pragmatic definition of physics by Franklin (1903) illuminating:

> I think that the sickliest notion of physics, even if a student gets it, is that it is "the science of masses, molecules and the ether." And I think that the healthiest notion, even if a student does not wholly get it, is that physics is *the science of the ways of taking hold of bodies and pushing them*! [emphasis added] (p. 15).

In order to develop a Pragmatic account of measurement, I would propose the following characterization of measurement in the same spirit as Franklin's definition of physics (1903):

> Measurement is (i) an activity of classification, ordination, or quantification of a set of elements (ii) according to a model (iii) of a relevant attribute (iv) in service of a larger goal.

4.1 Why an Activity? Why Three of Them?

Noting that measurement is an activity is not unique to this definition, as other definitions implicitly characterize measurement as an activity, either as *numerical estimation* (Michell 1997b, p. 383), *assignment of numerals* both by Campbell (1920, p. 267) and Stevens (1946, p. 677), or *obtaining and reasonably attributing* in the case of the VIM. The difference here lies simply in making it explicit to remind us that measurement is being conducted to engage with the world, not to passively mirror the world under the spectator theory of knowledge, but to support a successful use. Viewed in this light, a measurement need not be understood as replicating or recovering a set of *true* values, but as actively classifying, ordering, and quantifying.

In this proposed definition, I have included not one, but three types of activities: classification, ordering, and quantification. This is of course not a trivial issue, as a large part of the debate over the definition of measurement is related to this point (Fig. 4.1).

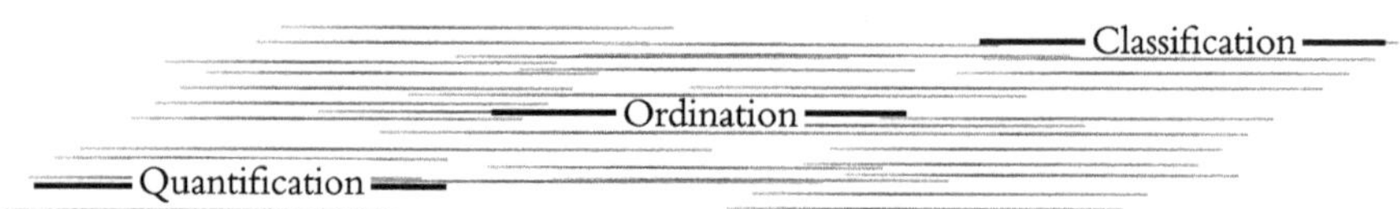

Fig. 4.1 Three fibers in the thread of measurement

To explain why it might be relevant to list these specific activities, it is important to consider the *level of the activities*. A simple example will suffice to clarify it. Let us take as an example "having dinner." There are many actions that could be used to describe what is occurring. While some may say I am having dinner, for instance, we could say more broadly that I am eating, that I am acquiring nutrients, or even that I am subsisting. We could, on the other hand, say more narrowly that I am sitting down, that I am reaching for food with my hands, or that I am chewing and swallowing. In this example, I think that "subsisting" is, for most purposes, too broad a level of description, and that "chewing and swallowing" is too narrow. I would argue that one of the main sources of confusion when discussing measurement is the different levels at which the activity of measurement is described, with most definitions focusing on too concrete a level by talking about "estimation," "assignment," "attribution," versus much more abstract alternative characterization such as "a central epistemic enterprise" (Trout 1998, p. 150).

I think that a more descriptive way of characterizing what we are attempting to achieve when we purport to conduct measurement is to describe measurement somewhere in between the too concrete and too abstract alternatives described above, hence classification, ordering, and quantification. The verbs more directly describe the outcomes that researchers and practitioners have in mind when they attempt to conduct a measurement. Distinguishing between these activities helps clarify whether we want to distinguishing differences of kind, order or quantity in the relevant attribute that we are measuring.

There are of course potentially infinite levels of distinctions that could be made regarding the activities that we engage in when measuring. However, it seems to me that the debate over the practice of measurement is concentrated on two main levels that are usually brought to bear in discussion regarding the definition of measurement. These levels are presented in Fig. 4.2.

On the left side Fig. 4.2, we have a higher-level activity, assessment, while on the right-hand side, we have another level with three, more concrete, activities: classification, ordering, and quantification. The lines in this diagram are meant to indicate not only that assessment is a higher-level activity than the other three but also that assessment can be considered as a lower-level concept of another activity (e.g., epistemic enterprise), and that each one of the lower-level activities included

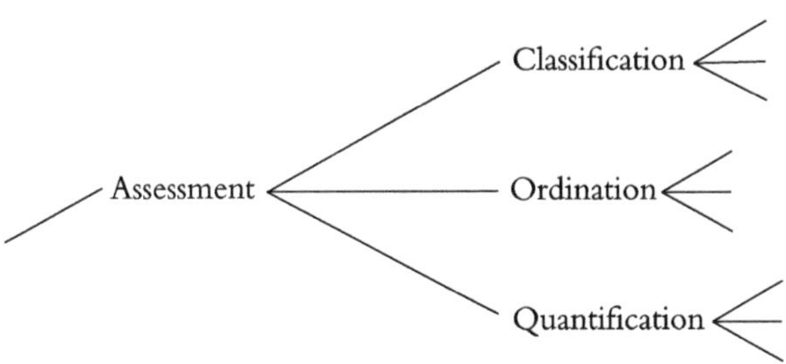

Fig. 4.2 Two possible uses of "Measurement"

in the diagram could in their own right be analyzed in lower-level actions (e.g., estimation, assignment).[1]

Measurement has purposefully been left out of this diagram because an important part of the debates regarding the concept of measurement is due to the conflict between approaches that attempt to establish measurement at the level comparable to assessment (e.g., most representational approaches), versus those that want to restrict to quantification (CTM), and perhaps, ordering (e.g., the current definition under the VIM). When viewed in this light, it is possible to think that we could avoid much disagreement by simply abandoning the word "measurement," and settling for the names in Fig. 4.2 or other similar ones; however, as there is considerable prestige in the name "measurement," it seems unlikely that researchers all over the world will simply decide to rechristen their practices.

However, as can be inferred from the inclusion of classification, ordering, and quantification in the definition above, if suddenly the entire world where to decide in this renaming effort, the title of this book could be simply be renamed to "A Pragmatic Perspective of Assessment."[2]

Why am I inclined toward a view of measurement as closer to assessment, or at the very least as broader than quantification? Because the attributes that interest us in the social sciences can be, in principle, modeled in any of these three ways, and I think that our study in all of these cases would benefit from a common framework that aspires to produce reliable and actionable knowledge. Purposefully prescribing walls between these traditions, and attempting to enforce them, is counterproductive to this agenda.

When studying an attribute of interest in the social sciences, such as proficiency in mathematics, we traditionally hypothesize that inter-individual differences can be well modeled in terms of quantitative differences. However, it is also possible to model these differences in terms of ordered levels of proficiency, or even, in some cases, as different kinds of approaches (e.g., solution strategies) adopted by the respondents. Each one of these models has different implications regarding the structure of the attribute of interest and different possible inferences that we can make about the persons that are being studied. When working to understand an attribute, we should avoid forcing *a priori* the selection of a continuous, ordinal, or categorical model.

The alternative is to emphasize the divide between them, developing a discipline of measurement, with its vocabulary and institutional knowledge solely for the scenario in which we want to model the attribute as quantitative. It is to have

[1]What about counting? From this PPM, there would not be an Aristotelian distinction between discrete and continuous quantities, therefore there would be no need to exclude a priori counting as a form of measurement.

[2]One difficulty not often discussed among proponents of the rechristening of some practices as "assessment" instead of "measurement" is the assumption that a comparable word at that level of generality exists in every language. This is by no means a given, and at least in Spanish, there is no separate word for "assessment" aside from words like *medición*, *evaluación*, and *valoración* that, respectively, would correspond to *measurement*, *evaluation*, and *valuation*.

a parallel methodological tradition solely dedicated to ordinal modeling and yet another one for classification, each one with its own lingo. I would argue that this has been the alternative favored so far. We have a psychological and educational measurement tradition dominated by the focus on modeling attributes as quantitative (Birnbaum 1968; Rasch 1960/1980), a separate tradition of practice that focuses on ordinal measures (Cliff & Keats 2003), and yet another methodological tradition and professional community focused on classification (Hagenaars & McCutcheon 2002; Lazarsfeld & Henry 1968). One possible, perhaps ideal, outcome of having these separate traditions could be that researchers in the social sciences could take advantage of the methodological expertise of any and all of them, freely exploring the alternative ways in which the attribute that they are studying could be structured. However, I do not think this is occurring. On the contrary, it seems that the association of the concept of measurement in the social sciences with one of these practices, quantification, in addition to the separation of these three traditions, hampers the flexibility of social scientists to consider alternative modeling practices of the attributes of interest. If one is taught classification methods, everything becomes a taxonomy; if one is taught continuous measurement models, everything looks like a number line.

To be clear, I do not think that separation between these research traditions is *per se* negative, or that specialization is a negative development. However, I do think that it is possible to do a better job relating these traditions, highlighting their family resemblances, and not limiting the way in which we conceptualize the attributes we study due to barriers in our methodological traditions. This is especially necessary as our statistical frameworks blur the distinction between these traditions. In this context, I think that understanding the concept of measurement at the level of "assessment" in Fig. 4.2, is a step in the direction of more methodological and conceptual flexibility in the social sciences.

4.2 Why According to a Model?

Another important aspect of the proposed definition makes explicit that the classification, ordering, or quantification of the elements of a set of elements is conducted *according to a model* of the attribute of interest. This model, usually a substantive scientific theory, is key, as it defines which objects can be conceived as having the attribute, establishes what kind of relations characterize the attribute, guides our expectations regarding potential study and manipulation (e.g., does it make sense to order it? can we calculate distances between different instances of the attribute?), and finally, provides the basis for justifying why the instrument or transducer[3] is an appropriate indicator of the attribute of interest.

One of the critical functions that is served by the model that we have of our attribute of interest is that it will constrain the level of precision to which we can interpret the results of our measurements. As Boring (1920) emphasized in the early twentieth century:

> But, if in psychology we must deal—and it seems we must—with abilities, capacities, dispositions and tendencies, the nature of which we can not accurately define, then *it is senseless to seek in the logical process of mathematical elaboration a psychologically significant precision that was not present in the psychological setting of the problem* [emphasis added]. Just as ignorance will not breed knowledge, so inaccuracy of definition will never yield precision of result. (p. 33)

A warning worth keeping in mind in the social sciences where concepts often seem to be—echoing Allport (1935) in his seminal discussion of attitudes—"measured more successfully than they are defined" (p. 828). A situation that should prompt researchers and practitioners to wonder about the criterion used for defining success.

More generally, the "theory-ladenness" of measurement, meaning "the pervasive use of theoretical assumptions in designing measurement apparatuses and interpreting their indications" (Tal 2013, pp. 1167–1168), and its complexities have been extensively discussed (see, for instance, Chang 1995; Kuhn 1961; Van Fraassen 2008), such that "contemporary scholarship has come to view measurement as theory dependent by default" (Tal 2013, p. 1168).

As Tal (2013) has pointed out, "contemporary studies show that theoretical and statistical models of a measurement process are necessary preconditions for obtaining meaningful measurement outcomes in the first place" (p. 1166). The role of models as part of measurement is featured across different measurement traditions, including the latent variable literature in general (Skrondal & Rabe-Hesketh 2004), and psychometrics in particular (Wilson 2013), as well as economics (Boumans 2001) and metrology (Mari 2003).

However, the inclusion of models of the attribute and models of the measurement process could raise a potential contradiction with the original Pragmatic emphasis on the abandonment of the mirroring metaphor for the practice of measurement. This contradiction would stem from maintaining the attachment to the spectator theory of knowledge and its commitment to the idea that models are supposed to be evaluated in terms of how closely they resemble reality. Teller (2001) describes this view of models, stating that "the photograph provides a good icon: The ambition has

---

[3] A measuring transducer is defined in the VIM as a devise, used in measurement, that provides an output quantity having a specified relation to the input quantity (Joint Committee for Guides in Metrology 2012).

been to produce a perfect likeness of nature, a perfect model." So, to recap, under this traditional spectator theory of knowledge we have a natural kind that is being represented (i.e., mirrored) by a model in one or more ways, where the adequacy of the model is judged in terms of how close our model resembles the aforementioned natural kind. However, we need not conceive models this way.

The next section will tackle an alternative to the notion of natural kind in favor of relevant ones, so the present question is, how can we judge the adequacy of a model in a way that does not depend on the idea of resemblance.

An example, consider the case in which you are interested in judging the quality of a set of models for the human heart. You are presented with four different models:

- The first one was created as an aid to explain hearts to middle school students.
- The second was created as an aid in training surgeons.
- The third model was created as a specification for creating an artificial heart.
- And the last model was created as a specification for cloning a heart replacement.

Does it make sense to ask which of these representations is the correct one? I think not. Does it make sense to answer this based on similarity with a canonical heart (whatever that means)? They all have some similarities, but none of them mirrors all of them. If you want me to find a heart in a human body, certain elements will be considered as establishing that resemblance. If I am blind, and you want me to identify it, then other elements would have to be communicated, and the figure that was useful for me, who can see, is no longer useful. As Nelson Goodman (1970) illustrates with a brief thought experiment:

> ... suppose we have three glasses, the first two filled with colorless liquid, the third with a bright red liquid. I might be likely to say the first two are more like each other than either is like the third. But it happens that the first glass is filled with water and the third with water colored by a drop of vegetable dye, while the second is filled with hydrochloric acid—and I am thirsty. Circumstances alter similarities. (p. 28)

The idea here is that even when modeling ostensibly the same object, a human heart, the idea that we can resort to resemblance as a criterion for model adequacy is a misleading one, as what counts as features that are to be mirrored in the model will vary significantly depending on the use that we want to give to the model. Additionally, it is unclear that a perfect reproduction would constitute a useful alternative. After all, a perfect reproduction would be a clone of what is being modeled, and as Lewis Carroll (1893) illustrates, this may not be a practical alternative:

> ".... What do you consider the *largest* map that would be really useful?"
> "About six inches to the mile."
> "Only *six inches!*" exclaimed Mein Herr. "We very soon got to six *yards* to the mile. Then we tried a *hundred* yards to the mile. And then came the

> grandest idea of all! We actually made a map of the country, on the scale of *a mile to the mile*!"
>
> "Have you used it much?" I enquired.
>
> "It has never been spread out, yet," said Mein Herr: "the farmers objected: they said it would cover the whole country, and shut out the sunlight! So we now use the country it-self, as its own map, and I assure you it does nearly as well. . . . " (p. 169)

Consider as another example the case of the attribute *college readiness*. We might consider this attribute, and be concerned about modeling it, because we do not want to send to college (nor fund) students that we think might not succeed there or finish their education. Alternatively, we might be concerned with the limited number of vacancies, and we want to make sure that those who can take the most advantage of them should be the ones selected to attend. Based on these or other concerns, we could think of multiple models of how this attribute may vary across individuals.

If our goal is selecting only those who are deemed "ready," regardless of the fact that those may be less than the amount of vacancies, we may think of college readiness as a binary attribute, such that any given person is either ready or not ready to succeed in college. Under this model, we can conceive of a qualitatively distinct class, the college-ready class of students, that is characterized by distinct academic, emotional and social attributes. We would therefore want to classify students as being members or not of this class.

If our goal is not only to select those who are ready, but also to offer different kinds of support activities targeted to students' strengths and weaknesses, we may think that college readiness is best modeled by multiple classes. Under this model, we can hypothesize that there is a first class of students who are ready for college because of their academic prowess, a second class of students whose college readiness is based on their emotional maturity, a third class that is characterized by good social skills, and finally, a fourth class of students that are not characterized by any of the previous profiles.

If all we want to do is fill the available vacancies, without any assumptions regarding the "absolute" level of readiness of the students, we could use an ordinal model. In this case we think that some students are overall "more ready" or "less ready" than others, and it is possible to order or rank them from 1 to N based on these more-or-less relations, and then count until we run out of vacancies.

Finally, if we think that there is a specific cutpoint that we consider to be "ready enough" (just like the height check before a roller coaster), we may think of college readiness as a continuous variable, very much like height, where we see each students' readiness as summarized in a single metric that allows quantitative comparisons among them. Alternatively, this last model would be very useful if, for instance, we had a well established function for manipulating college readiness, such that we could estimate the amount of additional hours/resources of training that would be required for the students to achieve such cutpoint.

Each one of these descriptions of the relevant attribute "college readiness" are in principle possible, and it is an empirical question whether they prove useful or not when put to work in a given context. It might be the case that more than one of these models proves fruitful, or perhaps none of them will. Nevertheless, what we are doing in these different cases is trying to classify, order or quantify inter-individual differences according to our model of this relevant attribute to accomplish a larger goal, as opposed to focusing on whether college readiness is truly a natural attribute, or if we should ban or not some of these models because they do not adequately capture the true nature of college readiness.

This point is more generally made by Rorty (1999) about objects but is equally valid for attributes:[4]

> No description of an object is more a description of the 'real', as opposed to the 'apparent', object than any other, nor are any of them descriptions of, so to speak, the object's relation to itself—of its identity with its own essence. Some of them are, to be sure, better descriptions than others. But this betterness is a matter of being more useful tools—tools which accomplish some human purpose better than do competing descriptions. All these purposes are, from a philosophical as opposed to a practical point of view, on a par. There is no over-riding purpose called 'discovering the truth' which takes precedence. As I have said before, pragmatists do not think that truth is the aim of inquiry. The aim of inquiry is utility, and there are as many different useful tools as there are purposes to be served. (p. 54)

In this sense, a model, like a theory and language in general, is also "an adaptation to the environment, a set of tools for dealing with the causal pressures exerted by the environment, rather than a way of mirroring it" (Tartaglia 2007, p. 214). As such, determining the adequacy of a model of a heart, a model of college readiness, or any other object or process will depend on our purpose given a context of application. This point has also been raised by Minsky (1968), where he defines a model by stating:

> To an observer B, an object A^* is a model of an object A to the extent that B can use A^* to answer questions that interest him about A. The model relation is inherently ternary. *Any attempt to suppress the role of the intentions of the investigator B leads to circular definitions or to ambiguities about "essential features" and the like.* [Emphasis added] (p. 426)

[4]Especially given Rorty's panrelational stance, where absent the idea of essential features, "there is nothing to be known about [objects] except an initially large, and forever expandable, web of relations to other objects. Everything that can serve as the term of a relation can be dissolved into another set of relations, and so on for ever. There are, so to speak, relations all the way down, all the way up, and all the way out in every direction: you never reach something which is not just one more nexus of relations." (pp. 53–54).

Echoing the words of Dewey, the quality of our model can be evaluated based on how good the model is at doing the kind of work that we need it to do for us.

This perspective offers us an amended version of Box' (1987) dictum "all models are wrong, but some are useful" (p. 424), which we could revise to indicate simply that *some models are useful.*[5]

4.3 Why a "relevant" Attribute?

Another aspect of the proposed definition that is worth highlighting is the explicit reference to *relevant attributes*. According to Webster's Third New International Dictionary, "relevant" is defined as:

> Bearing upon or properly applying to the matter at hand; affording evidence tending to prove or disprove the matters at issue or under discussion; PERTINENT

Relevant is used in this sense here to make a distinction from the idea of a *natural* attribute, either a kind and/or a universal. This distinction is in the same spirit as Nelson Goodman's (1975) distinction between *natural* and *relevant* kinds:

> I say 'relevant' rather than 'natural' for two reasons: first, 'natural' is an inapt term to cover not only biological species but such artificial kinds as musical works, psychological experiments, and types of machinery; and second, 'natural' suggests some absolute categorical or psychological priority, while the kinds in question are rather habitual or traditional or devised for a new purpose. (p. 63)

This distinction is apropos here to present an alternative to the idea that measurement must be concerned with natural kinds or universals. Metaphysical realism, where the commitment is to natural kinds and/or universals as opposed to relevant kinds and relevant attributes, is illustrated by Michell (2011, p. 252):

> Concepts are not tools, somehow already present in our minds and able to be imposed upon a non-conceptual reality, for good or ill. Rather, concepts are features of reality. For example, when I see that this rose is red, whatever it is *to be a rose* and *to be red* (i.e., the concepts involved) are real qualities, present in indefinitely many particular plants and indefinitely many physical objects. Otherwise I could never judge veridically that this rose is red—something I can surely do.

[5]Another revision to Box' famous quote, made in an akin spirit but from a different line of argumentation, was posed by Tarpey (2009), who proposes that "All models are right, [but] most are useless".

As it was discussed in Sect. 2.1 Michell's take on how attributes are part of reality is a central feature of the CTM, and his example about color illustrates the extent to which he thinks of science in general and measurement in particular as discovering reality itself, describing it in its natural state, untainted by human activity. For this reason, it is interesting to make a small aside and focus on an alternative to this "let's just carve nature at its joints" approach to color in particular and attributes in general.

Despite Michell's self-confidence in his capacity to correctly identify the colors as they are in reality itself, not everyone agrees with this bullish assessment:[6]

> Color concepts are "interactional"; they arise from the interactions of our bodies, our brains, the reflective properties of objects, and electromagnetic radiation. Colors are not objective; there is in the grass or the sky no greenness or blueness independent of retinas, color cones, neural circuitry, and brains. Nor are colors purely subjective; they are neither a figment of our imaginations nor spontaneous creations of our brains. (Lakoff & Johnson 1999, pp. 24–25)

Varela et al. (1991) examine in detail the issue of color as a cognitive phenomenon, discussing some of its neurological, physical, and conceptual aspects. In their review, they dispute the common assumption that there *must* be some physical correlate of colors, pointing out that:

> This relative independence of perceived color from locally reflected light has been known to vision scientists for quite some time. The independence is manifested in two complementary phenomena. In the first, the perceived colors of things remain relatively constant despite large changes in the illumination. This phenomenon is known as *approximate color constancy*. In the second, two areas that reflect the same spectral composition can be seen to have different colors depending on the surrounding in which they are placed. This phenomenon is known as *simultaneous color contrast* or *chromatic induction*. (p. 160)

Varela et al. go on to conclude their examination of color by indicating that "we can now appreciate, then, how color provides a paradigm of a cognitive domain that is neither pregiven nor represented but rather experiential and enacted" (p. 171). As Rorty (1999) points out:

> To say that *X* is really blue even though it appears yellow from a certain angle and under a certain light, is to say that the sentence '*X* is blue' is more useful—that is, can be employed more frequently—than the sentence

[6]On a personal note, being "colorblind" myself I have learned the hard way not to make those kinds of statements about color.

'*X* is yellow.' The latter sentence is useful only for occasional, evanescent purposes. (p. 51)

This aside about color is simply to illustrate a central aspect of the proposed PPM, and how it differs not only from the CTM but from all other approaches that, as characterized by Varela et al., emphasize the idea that in general "the world can be divided into regions of discrete elements and tasks," and, based on that premise, assert that "[cognition] must, if it is to be successful, respect the elements, properties and relations within these pregiven regions" (Varela et al. 1991, p. 147).

From a PPM, the emphasis is on the idea of relevant attributes, and relevant objects for that matter, that emerge from our practices and efforts to cope with the world. If you are wondering at this point about who determines what is relevant, Hacking (2007) answers, directly in relation to Goodman's concept of relevant kinds, "to us, or to you, or to them, to those who group items together, for this or that purpose. Relevance is all there is to be said, in general" (p. 46).

4.4 Why in Service of a Larger Goal?

The final, and perhaps crucial point raised in this proposed definition is the explicit characterization of measurement as a purposeful activity in service of a larger goal, highlighting that when engaged in measurement, we aim to accomplish something.

The reason for explicitly including goals in the definition is that, from a Pragmatic point of view, the goals provide the criteria for judging whether the measurement we are examining is a good one or a bad one depending on the extent that they help us accomplish them. Associating a measurement with a specific and explicit goal both (a) restricts its scope, hopefully tempering inferences and statements based on it, and (b) establishes the criteria by which the measurement is to be judged.

From a PPM, conducting a measurement is not an all-or-nothing proposition. Accepting the use of a procedure as a "measurement" is not an act of canonization that ensures that its results are always true, that it can be used in any context or that we can draw any inference from it. The question is not *is this truly measurement?*, but *is this a useful measurement for this explicit purpose?*

Although the inclusion of goals as an explicit part of the proposed pragmatic definition of measurement can seem controversial, the role of goals in measurement has traditionally been part of the discussion, albeit on the background.[7] Take, for instance, Campbell's position on the matter:

[7]An example of this controversy was the debate generated by the introduction of *Consequential Validity* as part of the 1999 Standards for Educational and Psychological Testing. See Sect. 5.1 for a discussion on this point.

> Measurement is only a means to an end; we want to express the properties of systems by numerals only because we are thereby enabled to state laws about them. (Campbell 1920, p. 328)

And, more recently, Michell (2008b, p. 137), discussing Denny Borsboom's book *Measuring the Mind*:

> This does not distinguish measurement from cognition generally, and it misses the main point of measurement, which is to get to know about *quantitative* attributes.

I contend that, while Campbell's and Michell's proposed definitions of measurement do not explicitly reference the goals of measurement as an activity, these quotes indicate that the goals that they consider for the practice of measurement are indeed strongly shaping their perspective on the matter. Campbell's stated goals conceive measurement as a means to formulate laws of nature, and Michell presents measurement as solely concerned with learning about quantities, in accordance with his alignment with the spectator theory of knowledge. Campbell places quite an onus on those that want to engage in measurement, you either come up with natural laws or go home. For Michell and his realist approach to measurement, the main aim is to address the scientific task of measurement, which centers on determining if something really is or not a quantity, a daunting and very specific proposition. The commonality between the two is that measurement is conceived as a purely research oriented enterprise and a very narrow one at that. Their characterizations of measurement are in service of restricting measurement exclusively to those practices that help them address those goals. Our definition of the goals of measurement will certainly constrain our definition of measurement, and more importantly, it will prime our interpretation of what we *should* expect from its outcomes. In the case of these narrow goals, the constraint seems to be: *measurement if and only if we make inferences about nature's laws*.

These are of course valid goals, but they are only *some* of the possible goals, not in principle better or worse than other goals. I contend that this appraisal of the goals of measurement is simply too narrow, excluding valuable reasons for attempting to measure, and I am not alone on this. In his paper, *On The Nature and Purpose of Measurement*, Ernst Adams (1966) presents a pragmatic friendly—though not explicitly so—take on this matter, contesting the focus on research as the sole purpose of measurement:

> My position emphasizes the role of measurement in *application*, where a theory may be involved, but the objective is to do something or anticipate something, and not to create or test a theory. A comprehensive theory of science should give both aspects of it their due, of course, yet it seems to me that much recent writing greatly overemphasizes the "inquiry" or research aspect perhaps derogating the applied aspect as "mere engineering". (p. 153)

The drift from conceiving measurement as a practical problem solving tool toward one that focused on theory building has also been noted by Duncan (1984, p. 2):

> What I am trying to suggest is that many—and perhaps the most basic—of the procedures natural and social scientists use in measuring were actually invented to solve practical problems. In the beginning, measurement served social purposes only. The scientist may come into the picture when there is a recognized need to improve the measuring instrument. Or, taking the current practice of measurement as his point of departure, he may let his imagination work freely on ideas of amount, extent, magnitude, intensity, duration, numerousness, dimension, scale, and proportion to create abstract conceptual structures and systems of relationships.

The connection with the problem solving focus of measurement is key in the context of this pragmatic framework because our goals are, in the most general sense, an expression of our need to adapt to the "causal pressures exerted by the environment" (Tartaglia 2007, p. 214).

This is, of course, not the first appeal to usefulness in relation to a goal as a criterion for measurement. For instance, Churchman (1959)—in a piece called *Why measure?*—presents a similar perspective: "Suppose, then, we propose that the function of measurement is to develop a method for generating a class of information that will be useful in a wide variety of problems and situations" (p. 84). From this proposal, he indicates:

> We can begin by noting one rather striking consequence of the proposal. The objective of measurement can be accomplished in a number of ways... The qualitative consignment of objects to classes and the assignment of numbers to objects are two means at the disposal of the measurer for generating broadly applicable information. But which means is better? The striking consequence of the proposal is that measurement is a decision making activity, and, as such, is to be evaluated by decision making criteria. (p. 84)

A few years later, Adams (1966) would similarly argue for the importance of the purpose of measurement (while making a case against the abstract focus of the representational theory of measurement):

> Though the work of Campbell and others in the representational tradition has contributed to our understanding of measurement, the proponents of this approach have neglected to consider what it is that measurements are made *for*, and in so doing have been led to conclusions as to what measurement *ought* to be which are in serious disagreement with what scientists do. (Adams 1966, p. 125)

Adams (1966) put forward what he called an "informational account of measurement" such that:

> ... measures of a quantity are not so much "true" or "false" as they are more or less informative about the phenomena which they are supposed to be indices of.

I, of course, think that Adams (1966) is onto something here, and I would simply suggest amending this to indicate that measurements are *more or less useful to the goal that we are trying to accomplish*. I think this modification would certainly be in the spirit of Adams' own treatment of measurement, as his discussion of the Mohs scale of hardness illustrates: "The two basic things to know about this measure are: (1) what it is used for, and (2) how it is made" (Adams 1966, p. 133). These are two questions that, from this Pragmatic Perspective of Measurement, everyone that purports to measure should answer about their measurement instruments.

Having argued for the importance of considering the larger goals of measurement, it is good to tackle directly some common objections to the inclusion of a pragmatic criterion such as this. A first concern is that considering a pragmatic criterion based on usefulness in relation to goals will endorse irrelevant goals. Take, for instance, Michell's objection on this regard:

> Utility is a relative notion, and not all kinds of utility are relevant to the scientific enterprise. For example, there are a number of senses in which quantitative methods can be said to work well in psychology. First, those who have employed them have often profited from doing so. The public is impressed, careers are advanced, and money is made. Second, some quantitative procedures have been found to enable moderately useful predictions of other events. However, criteria such as these are really irrelevant to the scientific enterprise. The only criterion of interest to the scientific enterprise as such is that of advancing investigations into the ways of working of things. (Michell 2003, p. 47)

Two points come to mind. First, the inclusion of goals as proposed by this PPM would explicitly deal with the case where someone purports to measure and claims that it is useful because he or she was able to get peer reviewed publications out of it; this is certainly a case that someone could make. However, the definition proposed here asks for an explicit declaration of the larger goals that the measurement is supposed to address, and though it is possible, it seems unlikely that someone would attempt to justify his or her practice by making that kind of claim. Even if someone were candid enough to justify it this way, we would immediately understand that the "measure" is at best of extremely limited interest and usefulness. Any expectations that we could have previously had regarding such a measurement are immediately tempered by the narrowness made explicit in the goal. But what about the case where a scholar simply wants to publish a paper with measurement to put some ideas "out there" so they can be part of the discussion? Would about that kind of utility? The question in this case would be, what is the role of the measurement claims in the paper. If the measurement claims are not central, or perhaps even accessory, then we can ask why they were included, but ultimately will evaluate the value of the new ideas outside a discussion about measurement. If on the other hand, the measurement claims are central, then the ideas in the paper are relevant to a measurement and should be examined accordingly. This is in the spirit of ceasing to consider "measurement" as a label—or a blessing—that ensures ultimate knowledge; we need to ask of each measurement, following Adams (1966), the details of both why it was made and how it was made.

Second, and going back to the point of how the adoption of an implicit "goal of measurement" informs different definitions of measurement, Michell's judgment regarding the irrelevance of "moderately useful predictions of other event" is predicated on a perspective of science in general, and measurement in particular, where you either figure out *the way things really work* or not: Did you discover truth about reality or not? is it really measurement or not? That is certainly one approach to valuing the practice of science and measurement, alternatively, this PPM would promote recognizing that such "moderately useful predictions" are more or less valuable depending on the context of application. Granted, a scale of clinical depression constructed under a measurement by fiat stance may not reveal ultimate truth about the quantitative or qualitative status of "depression" and may not allow us to formulate laws that reveals the underlying mechanics of depression, but if it allows therapists to reduce the rate of suicides among their patients, I for one would not qualify it as a useless outcome or that it is not of interest to psychological science. I contend that a criterion so stringent that would consider this as useless to science is predicated on the complete disconnect between the role of science and measurement with the practical concerns of human beings, which albeit is a possible stance, is contrary to the perspective advanced here.

Another issue that may raise concerns about the idea of pragmatic justification is that when it has been invoked in the past, it has been usually interpreted as allowing any kind of inference, past or future, about the attributes that are being measured. In this light pragmatic justification seems cheap, its criterion weak and too permeable. However, I contend that this is a product of a very specific interpretation, that I call the *"any use, any time"* approach to pragmatic justification, which basically assumes that the mere possibility of a use is enough to support any use. The problem with a *any use, any time* approach is that it seems just too lax; if taken to heart, mere possibility of some use, some time, under some unspecified context is justification enough: perhaps my anxiety questionnaire has no practical applications right now, but it might!

There is of course nothing wrong with entertaining potential future applications, I would simply argue that they should not be equated with actual applications, after all, many procedures could in the future be successfully used to classify, order or quantify under a certain context, but until that happens, claiming to have measured seems premature. In contrast to the *any use, any time* approach, pragmatic justification can be understood to be emphasizing that the successful measurement procedures are connected to clearly specified uses under clearly specified contexts of application.

Take, for instance, Lord and Novick (1968) justification of the assumption of a continuous variable underlying the performance of respondents in their classic book *Statistical Theories of Mental Test Scores* saying:

> This could be considered as an arbitrary strengthening of our model. However, *from a pragmatic point of view* the only meaningful evaluation of this procedure is one based on an evaluation of the usefulness of the resulting scale. If we construct a test score by counting up correct responses (zero-one scoring) and treating the resulting scale scores as having interval properties the procedure may or may not produce a good predictor of some criterion. (p. 22)

This is in principle consistent with pragmatic perspective presented here (although Lord & Novick appear to have been using the word *pragmatic* without a special commitment to the philosophical school), it clearly anchors the measurement claim of any given instrument to a specific purpose for which we are supposed to have empirical evidence that validates it as, for example, a predictor.[8] However, if we accept the *"any use, any time"* interpretation, then "the only meaningful evaluation of this procedure is one based on an evaluation of the usefulness of the resulting scale" becomes a trivial constraint, after all, I can always use an educational test to start a fire (any use) and I can always claim that is just not useful yet (any time). Although these examples may seem silly, they highlight that the problems with a pragmatic justification emerge when we forget that if a measure was justified for a given purpose in a specific context of application, any measurement claim and the inferences derived from it are also constrained to that purpose. In the future, other potential uses can emerge, potentially expanding the scope of the original measurement claims, but such expansion must be justified by showing actual "cash value," not merely on the basis of promissory notes and good intentions.

From the Pragmatic Perspective of Measurement advanced here, *a pragmatic justification is not a blank check on inference*. If we are to invoke pragmatic justifications, we should take them seriously. A pragmatic justification defines the goals we are trying to accomplish, guides our selection of the attributes of interest, informs the aspects of our models that are relevant, provides desiderata for evaluating whether our measurement is useful or not and, most importantly, anchors our inferences to the context of the goal that we have defined. Generic statements regarding unspecified practical applications aimed at justifying otherwise unwarranted inferences are simply poor pragmatic justifications. This kind of poor

[8]Although some, like Hand (2004) for example, insist that pragmatic criteria are limited to prediction, there is in principle no reason for such limitation. A pragmatic perspective can seek, for instance, manipulation or explanation.

justification is made worse when the "pragmatism" is restricted solely to the methods section, but the conclusions are written as if by a metaphysical realist.

What does a pragmatic, contextualized, justification of a measurement looks like? We can find one in the history of intelligence measurement. Allow me to start with a brief digression on the work that Alfred Binet, usually considered the father of intelligence measurement and testing, had done on the topic of psychological measurement before working on the field of intelligence (cf. Michell 2012b). While studying the possibility of measuring suggestibility through an experiment involving the judgment of line lengths, Binet (1900)[9] had explicitly differentiated between quantitative measurement and ordering:

> All physical measurement, when it is precise, gives not only an ordering of measured objects, but furthermore an indication of the number of times that one object is larger, heavier, etc. than another, that is, an indication of the number of times that such a quantity contains the unit. This is not the same in psychological measurement; also, I think that this is not true measurement; it is quite simply ordering.[10] (pp. 103–104)

Why is it relevant that Binet made this distinction? This will become apparent presently, please bear with me. Years later, when presenting his effort (in collaboration with Simon) in the construction of an intelligence scale, Binet and Simon (1916) begin by stating in the first line of their article (in language common to their times):

> *Before explaining these methods let us recall exactly the conditions of the problem which we are attempting to solve* [emphasis added]. Our purpose is to be able to measure the intellectual capacity of a child who is brought to us in order to know whether he is normal or retarded. We should therefore, study his condition at the time and that only. We have nothing to do either with his past history or with his future...

It was in the context of making diagnostic decisions of students in primary school, and with that goal in mind, that Binet and Simon (1916) state:[11]

> This scale properly speaking does not permit the measure of the intelligence, because intellectual qualities are not superposable, and therefore cannot be measured as linear surfaces are measured, but are on the

[9]There is no current English translation of this book. I thank Rebecca Freund for kindly translating the relevant passages discussed here.

[10]In the original French Binet uses the word *classement*, which can mean, depending of the context either classification or ordering, and the context of this passage seems to be used in this last sense.

[11]This quote was brought to my attention by the detailed analysis that Michell (2012b) makes of it and its relation to the concept of heterogeneous orders, although he draws markedly different conclusions from it.

> contrary, a classification, a hierarchy among diverse intelligences; *and for the necessities of practice this classification is equivalent to a measure* [emphasis added]. (Binet & Simon 1916, pp. 40–41)

This is where the first quote about quantitative measurement and ordering becomes relevant. Although it did not make it to the English translation, Binet includes in the original French[12] a footnote to the word "measure," explicitly referencing his previous treatment of quantitative and ordinal attributes cited above. Binet understood the distinction between quantification and ordination, and while he acknowledged it, he stated that "for the necessities of practice"—which he made explicit in the first line of the article—his scale can be used for measurement. Here Binet proposed an ordinal scale of intelligence to be used for diagnostic decisions of students in primary school in the early twentieth century France, and provided evidence to support that use.

Binet was not measuring "Intelligence" as a universal variable, his focus was not the formulation of psychological laws, and he embarked in the construction of an ordinal measure to address a practical challenge. According to the pragmatic criterion proposed in this book, there is no such thing as an "Intelligence Measure" without a qualification of the context in which it is supposed to be useful. This raises the question of how to define a context, and what makes a context A similar enough to context B to justify the use of a measurement instrument developed for A applicable to B, or what makes context C different enough to make such a transfer questionable. Defining what is relevant or irrelevant in a context is not a trivial task, and arguments for or against of using an instrument in a new context will need to be examined in a case by case basis; then again, this kind of thoughtful consideration is already advocated, for instance, in the *Standards for Educational and Psychological Testing* (AERA et al. 1999, 2014).

If like Binet, we are engaged in solving a specific diagnostic or selection issue, our evaluation of that measurement should be according to that purpose, and the extent of our inferences should be also constrained to that purpose. If psychologists want to conceptualize and measure intelligence as an attribute akin to temperature, and/or as part of a set of psychological laws, certainly an ambitious goal, they will need to go beyond the evidence that Binet used to justify his measure, showing that "Intelligence" does behave in law-like relations—just like temperature does–with other attributes that have been quantified. As Sherry (2011) so clearly states:

> Acceptance of the pragmatic approach to quantification does not, of course, entail the existence of quantitative psychological attributes. *The pragmatic value must be demonstrated* [emphasis added]. The conceptual advance that we admired in temperature measurement has no obvious analogue in, for instance, intelligence measurement. The general intelligence

[12]In the original French this quote also uses the word *classement*, but in this case the English translation treats it as "classification" instead of "ordering." In light of the omitted footnote and the overall context, it is more likely that Binet meant "ordering" instead.

factor, g, does not occur in psychological laws in the straightforward way that temperature occurs in $m_1c_1(t_1 - t_f) = m_2c_2(t_f - t_2)$ and $\Delta Q = mc\Delta t$. g correlates mathematically with academic success, income, etc., but it is not clear that the correlation provides greater understanding when g is treated as cardinal rather than ordinal data.

Before this kind of evidence is brought to bear, our measures of intelligence are tailored, and anchored, to more modest goals. To those interested in creating measures for establishing quantitative psychological or social laws, I wish them well—and borrowing a phrase from Duncan (1984, p 170)—"I shall be interested in seeing the results but will only insist that a program not be mistaken for the accomplishment."

Chapter 5
Contrasting and Comparing

In this chapter I will discuss how the pragmatic definition of measurement proposed earlier compares to the other definitions explored in Chap. 2 by looking into the four components of this definition, namely the goal of measurement, the activities involved in it, the nature of the attribute, and the model of the attribute.

5.1 The Goals of Measurement

Perhaps the clearest difference from the Pragmatic definition versus the alternative definitions reviewed so far is the explicit inclusion of the goals of measurement as part of the definition. Neither the main theories—classical, operational, representational—nor the two application-oriented approaches—latent variables and metrology—discuss goals as an integral part of the definition of measurement.

As pointed out in Sect. 4.4, although the goals of measurement are not discussed as part of these definitions, measurement scholars often discuss what they consider to be the goals of measurement as part of the background to their definitions. In this sense, the unstated goals shape the definitions of measurement of different approaches.

In the case of Michell and the CTM, the goals of measurement, and science more generally, fall clearly within the tradition of the spectator theory of knowledge, with science aiming to "discover nature's way of working" (Michell 1990, p. 27), and measurement aiming to "get to know about *quantitative* attributes" (Michell 2008b, p. 137). This emphasis on measurement as portrayal is shared by the RMT tradition, where the focus is "how numbers enter into science" (Narens & Luce 1986, p. 166), attempting on the one hand "to understand the nature of empirical observations that can be usefully recoded, in some reasonably unique fashion, in terms of familiar mathematical structures" (Luce & Suppes 2002, p. 1), while on the other hand

D. Torres Irribarra, *A Pragmatic Perspective of Measurement*, SpringerBriefs in Psychology, https://doi.org/10.1007/978-3-030-74025-2_5

attempting to identify laws—in the same way as Campbell (1920)—based on the application of these mathematical structures (Luce & Suppes 2002; Narens & Luce 1986).

Again, notice that all these discussions about the goals of measurement, and the relation to the goals of science are not explicitly part of the definitions of measurement either in CMT and RMT. These discussions take place in introductions and backgrounds, and in these cases focus on *the* goal of measurement, shaping the respective measurement definitions and theories in ways that completely ignore different goals of measurements as a relevant aspect.

Adams' (1966) criticism of RMT for ignoring what measurements are made *for* is equally applicable to the CTM, as both of these theories appear to be solely concerned with what measurement ought to be in order to adequately create theories within research contexts, while disregarding practical ones. In other words, CMT and RMT as theories are shaped by their assumption that there can only be one goal for any and all measurements, namely the discovery of reality's laws.

For its part, measurement under operationalism as advocated by Dingle (1950) was ultimately concerned with the establishment of correlations "so as to afford a true picture of the relations which the observations exhibit" (p. 5). For Dingle, and presumably for Bridgman too, these correlations would no longer be simply a function of the external world, as they would depend on the operations performed to investigate them. However, despite this departure from the focus on the accurate portrayal of the world in CMT and RMT, operationalism simply transfers the idea of portrayal from the attempt to capture a single reality to the attempt to accurately portray the correlation of observations that emerge as a function of certain operations. In this version of operationalism, there is again a single overarching goal (which is much more general than in the previous two theories) that all measurements are after: "the process of measurement is specified only in those details which are necessary to ensure that the results obtained are useful for our ultimate purpose of correlation" (Dingle 1950, p. 14). Although in Dingle's operationalism the definition of measurement is so broad that it effectively it barely tells us what measurement should be, it stills frames measurement as a single purpose activity, in this case the very broad search for correlations.

In the case of the two application-oriented approaches, what measurements are made *for* is still not explicit in their definitions, but it is discussed actively in the surrounding context.

Given its close ties with statistical modeling, within the LVM tradition, the goal of measurement can often be conceived as the search for "good fit" between the statistical model and the data. However, this is by no means a unanimous perspective among those who rely on latent variable models in measurement contexts (Mislevy & Haertel 2006; Rasch 1960/1980; Wilson 2005; Wright 1997). Moreover, the professional communities that rely on these models to serve the public and inform policy—in addition to conducting research—have actively tackled the issue of the intended use of measurements. This concern hit the mainstream psychological and educational assessment community in the 1980s with the publication of the

1989 chapter on validity by Samuel Messick (1989) in the book *Educational Measurement*. This publication strongly emphasized a perspective where:

> ... the key issues of test validity are the interpretability, relevance, and utility of scores, the import or value implications of scores as a basis for action, and the functional worth of scores in terms of the social consequences of their use. (Messick 1989, p. 13)

This emphasis on the intended use and the consequences of measurement was later on incorporated into the 1999 *Standards for Educational and Psychological Testing*, a consensus document generated by three major professional associations: The American Educational Research Association (AERA), The American Psychological Association (APA), and the National Council for Measurement in Education (NCME).

In the face of the recognition that this perspective has achieved, it seems surprising to have previously declared that in the realm of latent variable modeling in particular, or in educational and psychological assessment in general, there is no explicit consideration of the goals—what measurements are for—in this approach. The reason for this seeming incongruence is that these two documents refer explicitly to the intended use of *tests and test scores*, which is used more or less interchangeably with measurement. As Maul (2014) indicates in his review of the 2014 version of the *Standards*:

> The term "measurement" is used throughout the Standards, but it is never defined; it appears to be used interchangeably with the terms "testing" and "assessment." Such an omission and identification could only be considered defensible if the concept of measurement had been thoroughly established to be synonymous with that of testing, but this is patently not the case, as has been pointed out repeatedly by others (e.g., Borsboom 2009; Hood 2009; Michell 1999).

The ambiguous, and potentially misleading, identification of testing and measurement is a symptom of the larger disconnect between practitioners of educational assessment and the larger measurement literature, such that measurement as a concept is defined separately (usually following Stevens' 1946 definition) from the concept of validity, in which the role of the intended use has been incorporated.

Finally, in the case of metrology, the goals of measurement are referenced in one of the three notes that complement the definition of measurement in the VIM (Joint Committee for Guides in Metrology 2012), where it is stated that "measurement presupposes a description of the quantity commensurate with *the intended use of a measurement result*, a measurement procedure, and a calibrated measuring system operating according to the specified measurement procedure, including the measurement conditions." [emphasis added] (p. 16). In this way, what measurements are made for (i.e., "the intended use of a measurement result") is dealt with in the same level as the other more engineering-related aspects of measurement.

Table 5.1 Comparison between theories—goals of measurement

	CTM	OPER.	RMT	LVM	METR.	PPM
Role	Implicit	Implicit	Implicit	Acknowledged	Acknowledged	Central
Goal	Discovery	Correlation	Find Laws	Intended use	Intended use	Intended use
Scope	Single	Single	Single	Multiple	Multiple	Multiple

The differences between these theories and this PPM regarding the goals of measurement are summarized in Table 5.1, indicating the role that goals play in the theory, what is the goals that are considered, and whether measurement is conceived to be a single or multiple goal activity.

Table 5.1 highlights that an important difference between this PPM is that the goals of measurement play a central role, being explicitly incorporated as part of the proposed definition of measurement. This contrast is stark against the implicit influence that the goals of measurement have in CTM, operationalism, and RMT, where the authors do not consider them as part of their definition of measurement. Within application-oriented theories, on the other hand, the role of measurement goals has been acknowledged to different extents, but it has not been incorporated as a central part of the measurement definition, with Metrology almost doing so by acknowledging the role of intended use in one of the notes that accompany the VIM definition.

5.2 The Activities of Measurement

As pointed out in Sect. 4.1, many if not all of the definitions of measurement discussed in this book describe it as some kind of activity. The central point that differentiates the proposed PPM is the emphasis on what I contend is a more useful level of description of the activities that we engage in when we want to measure, namely quantification, ordination and classification. This level of activities contrasts with the characterization in the other theories, such as *numerical estimation* in the CTM (Michell 1997b) or *numerical assignment* both in the RTM (Campbell 1920; Stevens 1946) and LVM, as well as *numerical production*—as a function of a set of operations—in operationalism (Dingle 1950). The closest definition in terms of the level of description of the activities is perhaps the one offered by Metrology, where the activities that are indicated in the definition correspond to "obtaining and reasonably attributing quantity values" (Joint Committee for Guides in Metrology 2012).

Despite the difference in the level of description of the activity, it is possible to examine which of the three activities that are explicitly identified in this PPM are consistent with the different theories reviewed in this book. A comparison regarding the activities of measurement between these theories and the PPM presented in this book is presented in Table 5.2.

Table 5.2 Comparison between theories—activities of measurement

	CTM	OPER.	RMT	LVM	METR.	PPM
Activity	Numerical estimation	Numerical production	Numerical assignment	Numerical assignment	Obtain and attribute quantity values	Quantification, ordination, and classification
Quantification	Yes	Yes	Yes	Yes	Yes	Yes
Ordination	No	Yes	Yes	Yes	Yes	Yes
Classification	No	Yes	Yes	Yes	No	Yes

In this sense, the most restrictive perspective is advocated by the CTM, where it is clear that only one of them—quantification—is rightfully considered as measurement. Both ordination and classification deal with qualitative distinctions and are better left to be examined through other—non-measurement related—means. All the other theories of measurement here reviewed adopt more expansive definitions, including at least ordination as part of measurement.

Among the theories that favor the inclusion of both quantification and ordination, but leave out classification, we can find the metrological definition found on the VIM (Joint Committee for Guides in Metrology 2012), where they strike an interesting middle ground: only quantities can be measured, but they include "ordinal quantities" in that group. Although none other of the main theories reviewed in this book subscribe just to the exclusion of classification as a form of measurement, this position can be found among other measurement scholars, being subscribed, for example, by Torgerson (1958), Berka (1983), and Duncan (1984).

The remainder of the theories reviewed in this book would more or less explicitly accommodate classification, ordination and quantification as part of measurement. Operationalism, at least as discussed by Dingle (1950), recognizes that some operation will generate a number, but it does not prescribe or limit them in any way, which in principle would allow quantification, ordination and classification (among other possible activities) as long as they are conceived as a set of operations. The representational measurement theory, ranging from Stevens (1946) to Narens and Luce (1986), through its focus on scales of measurement, effectively encompasses all three of the activities too. However, it is important to note that RMT is not really predicated over the distinction of activities at the level of quantification, ordination and classification, but on groups of mathematical transformation, which define many possible scales, including some that could arguably be located in between them, for example, the hyper-ordinal scale (Suppes & Zinnes 1962). It is worth mentioning though that classification, associated with nominal scales in RMT is hardly discussed in this literature (they are barely mentioned once by Krantz et al. in the first volume of *Foundations of Measurement*, for instance), presumably because they are of less interest mathematically speaking. Finally, Latent Variable Models in general encompass statistical models that support all three of these activities, but are not limited to them.

5.3 The Attributes We Measure

The nature of the attributes that are measured is another facet that differentiates the proposed PPM from the other theories discussed here. To illustrate this contrast, consider that the CMT—as proposed by Michell—construes measurement as the estimation of ratios of magnitudes which are part of reality, independent of any context or operations used to measure, while Operationalism—as proposed by Dingle—abandons the assumption of an underlying attribute and focus exclusively on the operations that are used to measure. Put a different way, for CTM the ratios that we want to estimate exist independent of what we do, while for Operationalism, the attributes that we want to measure are a product of what we do.

From the theories that were reviewed in Sect. 2, CMT has an explicit realist position about the attributes that are measured, having something to say about their ontology. In addition to CTM, and although not explicitly committed to realism, the language used in Metrology to define quantities seems clearly realist: "property of a phenomenon, body, or substance, where the property has a magnitude that can be expressed as a number and a reference" (Joint Committee for Guides in Metrology 2012, p. 2). This is not surprising considering that the Metrological community has been traditionally associated with the physical sciences, where realism seems to be the default position.

For their part, both Operationalism and RMT are different flavors of empiricism, and as such, they either stay away from ontological discussions in the case of RMT, or completely disavow them, as is the case of Operationalism. For RMT, all we have is qualitative data that we observe, and mathematical structures that we impose on them, without any discussion about the ultimate reality (or lack-thereof) of those observations. Operationalism for its part was conceived by Bridgman as a way of inoculating science from unstated ontological assumptions that could lead it astray, and therefore treated any talk about the underlying properties merely as a time-saving convenience at best. It is worth mentioning, however, that although these theories in their pure form may be incompatible with realism, that does not mean that they are always treated separately in practice. The mathematical developments of RMT have been accepted and incorporated as part of realist theories, as is the case for Michell (1990, 1999, 2005) and others. As Tal (2015) points out:

> While their stance towards operationalism and conventionalism is largely critical, realists are more charitable in their assessment of mathematical theories of measurement. Brent Mundy (1987) and Chris Swoyer (1987) both accept the axiomatic treatment of measurement scales, but object to the empiricist interpretation given to the axioms by prominent measurement theorists like Campbell (1920) and Ernest Nagel (1931, Cohen and Nagel 1934: Ch. 15).

At the same time, Operationalism has been adopted in social sciences, and particularly psychology, through the idea of "operational definition" while ignoring

Table 5.3 Comparison between theories—attributes

	CTM	OPER.	RMT	LVM	METR.	PPM
Attributes	Quantities	Results of operations	Observed qualitative data	Constructs	Quantities and ordinal quantities	Relevant attributes

its philosophical background, such that it can be used in methodology sections that support realist conclusions.

The LVM tradition is perhaps the most clearly agnostic perspective regarding the nature of the attributes that are measured, where the label *construct* can be used to refer to diametrically opposed interpretations of the models used for measurement (Table 5.3).

On one extreme, latent variable models can be understood as methods of data reduction, where we are simply reducing the complexity of multiple observed variables by calculating a more manageable summary, the latent variable. From this perspective, the latent variable does not represent an underlying attribute present in the world, but is simply a convenient summary. On the other extreme, latent variable models are to be understood from a realist perspective (Borsboom 2005; Borsboom et al. 2003):

> Entity realism about latent variables is needed to motivate the choice for the reflective model over the formative model. Theory realism follows from the observation that the formal side of the theory implies that it is possible to be wrong about the position of a subject on the latent variable, and that weaker formulations—using empirical adequacy instead of truth—are difficult to interpret. (p. 216)

5.4 The Model of the Attribute

As indicated in Sect. 4.2, in this book, the model of the attribute refers to the theory that defines which objects can be conceived as having the attribute, establishes what kind of relations characterize the attribute, guides our expectations regarding potential study and manipulation, and provides the basis for justifying why an instrument is an appropriate indicator of the attribute of interest. Although all the measurement theories discussed here recognize the role theories play in some or all of these aspects, they do not all agree on the prominence that these models play in their measurement definitions or the role that these theories have in the process of measurement.

A first element to note regarding the role of models is that both CMT and RMT have been traditionally uninterested in the details of how the theoretical models interact with the engineering aspects of measurement (i.e., the *instrumental task* of

Table 5.4 Comparison between theories—models

	CTM	OPER.	RMT	LVM	METR.	PPM
Level	Abstract	Instrumental	Abstract	Instrumental	Mixed	Mixed
Models	Descriptions	Eclectic	Descriptions	Eclectic	Eclectic	Tools

measurement for Michell, as opposed to the *scientific task*). As Tal (2015) points out when discussing the process of instrument calibration "traditional philosophical accounts such as mathematical theories of measurement do not elaborate on the assumptions, inference patterns, evidential grounds or success criteria associated with such methods." As such, these two approaches favor an abstract approach to measurement. This tendency of CMT and RMT contrasts with the opposite emphasis in operationalism and the approaches in the applied realm, where there seems to be a great deal of emphasis regarding the instrumental aspects of measurement. Although the introduction of this PPM has focused on the more philosophical aspects of measurement, the instrumental aspects are acknowledged as part of the model of the attribute, the selection of the procedure for quantification, ordination, and classification, as well as the goals of measurement. In this sense, this PPM follows Adams that "the two basic things to know about this measure are: (1) what it is used for, and (2) how it is made" (Adams 1966, p. 133).

Table 5.4 summarizes the differences between these theories and the PPM presented here in terms of their conceptualization of models. Both in terms of the level at which the models are specified and the role that the models play in them.

The focus on the instrumental aspects is a characteristic of Operationalism, where the operations involved in the measurement process constitute in themselves the attribute that is measured. For their part, the VIM in the field of Metrology and in the *Standards* in the fields of educational and psychological measurement also cover the instrumental aspects, with the *Standards* focusing solely on them and the VIM and GUM covering both the conceptual as well as instrumental aspects.

A second element when contrasting the role of models between these approaches is the role that the model is playing. For CTM, theories are attempts at descriptions of reality, and are usually not discussed in terms of models by Michell (1999, 2005). A similar role of description is played by substantive theory in RMT, where the aim is not to achieve an accurate description of an underlying reality, but to faithfully represent the relations observed in data. To the extent that CTM or RMT would consider that models play a role in measurement, these models would be considered descriptions, the former of reality, and the latter of observed data. This emphasis on *models as descriptions* is in contrast with an emphasis on *models as tools*, that while is not explicitly adopted in Operationalism, LVM or Metrology, is potentially consistent with them. In this sense, the PPM adopts the *models as tools* perspective, in accordance with the anti-representationalism characteristic of Pragmatism.

5.5 Summary

I have advanced a proposal for extending pragmatic ideas into the field of measurement, these ideas are organized in relation to a pragmatic definition of measurement presented in Sect. 4:

> Measurement is an activity of classification, ordination, or quantification of a set of elements according to a model of a relevant attribute in service of a larger goal.

In keeping with the pragmatic ideas presented in Sect. 1.1, this definition is provided as a tool. This particular tool is aimed at gauging measurement claims in terms of their usefulness in the face of the diversity of practices that are conducted under the banner of "measurement."

At the same time I cannot stress enough that this definition, and the set of questions that it attempts to raise, are not—nor pretend to be—exhaustive. One major issue, the specifics of the how and all the details of instrumentation, merits its own investigation, especially considering that each prototypical conception of measurement will likely carry its own standards for analyzing measurement methodologies.

Having said that, this PPM is not solely restricted to the criterion of utility, but also presents a pragmatic account of the attributes that we try to measure. I advocate that it is in our best interest to consider attempts to classify, order and quantify as prominent activities, in service of the different models that we can develop in our attempts to study, predict and manipulate the attributes that we consider relevant.

Going back to the imaginary dialog presented at the very beginning of this book, when presented with a measurement claim such as "I measured anxiety?," the PPM invites the skeptic to stop asking "did the researcher *really* measure anxiety?," and ask instead:

- What were you doing? Classifying, Ordering or Quantifying?
- What is the attribute that you were measuring?
- What is the model that you have of that attribute?

and last, but certainly not least:

- For what purpose are you measuring this attribute?

These are questions that can provide us with a general understanding of what is behind that measurement claim, clarifying what the attribute is supposed to be and what are the criteria for success according to the purpose of the measurement. While some may argue that this is too broad a definition, I would respond, that this definition is tailored to those that are more interested in understanding the what, the how and the why of the practices commonly referred to as measurement, than those whose focus is in elucidating whether each one of them *really* is or not measurement.

It is my hope that this PPM contributes to a better understanding between researchers, practitioners, and users of measurement, by bringing to the foreground an understanding of measurement where measures are not always concerned with quantification, that attributes need not be considered as natural kinds or universals, that understanding the model of the attribute that underlies a measurement is central to designing and interpreting measurements, and that the purpose for which the measurement was developed informs us about the scope of its utility, both to judge its success as well as limiting the inferences that can be supported by it.

References

Adams, E. W. (1965). Elements of a theory of inexact measurement. *Philosophy of Science, 32*(3/4), 205–228.

Adams, E. W. (1966). On the nature and purpose of measurement. *Synthese, 16*(2), 125–169.

Adams, E. W. (1979). Measurement theory. In P. Asquith & H. Kyburg (Eds.), *Current research in philosophy of science* (pp. 207–227). East Lansing, MI: Philosophy of Science Association.

AERA, APA, & NCME. (1999). *Standards for educational and psychological testing*. Washington, DC: American Psychological Association.

AERA, APA, & NCME. (2014). *Standards for educational and psychological testing*. Washington, DC: American Psychological Association.

Allport, G. W. (1935). Attitudes. In C. Murchison (Ed.), *A handbook of social psychology* (pp. 798–844). Worcester, MA: Clark University Press.

Aristotle. (2001). Categories. In R. McKeon (Ed.), *The basic works of Aristotle* (pp. 7–37). New York: Modern Library.

Armstrong, D. M. (1987). Comments on Swoyer and Forge. In J. Forge (Ed.), *Measurement, realism and objectivity* (pp. 311–317). Holland: Reidel.

Bacon, M. (2012). *Pragmatism: An introduction*. Malden, MA: Polity.

Berka, K. (1983). *Measurement: Its concepts, theories, and problems*. Dordrecht: Reidel.

Bernstein, R. J. (1998). Community in the pragmatic tradition. In M. Dickstein (Ed.), *The revival of pragmatism: New essays on social thought, law, and culture* (pp. 141–156). Durham: Duke University Press.

Bernstein, R. J. (2010). *The pragmatic turn*. Cambridge, UK; Malden, MA: Polity Press.

Binet, A. (1900). *La suggestibilité*. Paris: Schleicher frères.

Binet, A., & Simon, T. (1916). *The development of intelligence in children* (E. Kite, Trans.). Baltimore: Williams & Wilkins Company.

Birnbaum, A. (1968). Some latent trait models and their use in inferring an examinee's ability. In F. M. Lord & M. R. Novick (Eds.), *Statistical theories of mental test scores* (pp. 395–479). Reading, MA: Addison-Wesley.

Boring, E. G. (1920). The logic of the normal law of error in mental measurement. *The American Journal of Psychology, 31*(1), 1–33.

Boring, E. G. (1921). The stimulus-error. *The American Journal of Psychology, 32*(4), 449–471.

Boring, E. G. (1961). The beginning and growth of measurement in psychology. In H. Woolf (Ed.), *Quantification: A history of the meaning measurement in the natural and social sciences* (pp. 108–127). Indianapolis: Bobbs-Merrill.

Borsboom, D. (2005). *Measuring the mind: Conceptual issues in contemporary psychometrics*. Cambridge, New York: Cambridge University Press.

D. Torres Irribarra, *A Pragmatic Perspective of Measurement*, SpringerBriefs in Psychology, https://doi.org/10.1007/978-3-030-74025-2

Borsboom, D. (2009). Educational measurement, 4th edition: Book re- view. *Structural Equation Modeling, 16*, 702–711

Borsboom, D., Mellenbergh, G. J., & van Heerden, J. (2003). The theoretical status of latent variables. *Psychological Review, 110*(2), 203–219.

Boumans, M. (2001). Measure for measure: How economists model the world into numbers. *Social Research, 68*(2), 427–453.

Boumans, M. (2007). *Measurement in economics: A handbook*. London: Academic.

Box, G. E. P., & Draper, N. R. (1987). *Empirical model-building and response surfaces*. New York: Wiley.

Brandom, R. (2003). *Articulating reasons: An introduction to inferentialism*. Cambridge: Harvard University Press.

Brennan, R. L. (Ed.). (2006). *Educational measurement*. Westport, CT: Praeger Publishers.

Bridgman, P. W. (1927). *The logic of modern physics*. New York: Macmillan Co.

Bureau International des Poids et Mesures. (2014). What is Metrology? Retrieved October 12, 2014, from http://www.bipm.org/en/worldwide-metrology/

Campbell, N. R. (1920). *Physics: The elements*. Cambridge: University Press.

Campbell, N. R. (1928). *An account of the principles of measurement and calculation*. London: Longmans, Green and Co.

Campbell, N. R. (1940). Notes on Physical Measurement. *The Advancement of Science, 1*(2), 340–342.

Carroll, L. (1893). *Sylvie and Bruno concluded*. London: Macmillan and Co.

Chang, H. (1995). Circularity and reliability in measurement. *Perspectives on Science, 3*, 153–172.

Chang, H. (2009). Operationalism. Retrieved October 12, 2014, from http://plato.stanford.edu/entries/operationalism/.

Churchman, C. W. (1959). Why measure. In C. W. Churchman & P. Ratoosh (Eds.), *Measurement: Definitions and theories*. London: John Wiley & Sons.

Cliff, N. (1992). Abstract measurement theory and the revolution that never happened. *Psychological Science, 3*(3), 186–190.

Cliff, N., & Keats, J. A. (2003). *Ordinal measurement in the behavioral sciences*. Mahwah, NJ: Lawrence Erlbaum Associates.

Crocker, L. M., & Algina, J. (1986). *Introduction to classical and modern test theory*. New York: Holt, Rinehart, and Winston.

Croon, M. (1990). Latent class analysis with ordered latent classes. *British Journal of Mathematical and Statistical Psychology, 43*(2), 171–192.

Croon, M. (1991). Investigating Mokken scalability of dichotomous items by means of ordinal latent class analysis. *British Journal of Mathematical and Statistical Psychology, 44*(2), 315–331.

Croon, M. (2002). Ordering the classes. In J. A. Hagenaars & A. L. McCutcheon (Eds.), *Applied latent class analysis* (pp. 137–162). New York: Cambridge University Press.

Dawes, R., & Smith, T. (1985). Attitude and opinion measurement. In G. Lindzey & E. Aronson (Eds.), *The handbook of social psychology* (Vol. I, pp. 509–566). Hillsdale, NJ: Lawrence Erlbaum.

de Ayala, R. J. (2009). *The theory and practice of item response theory*. New York: Guilford Press.

Dewey, J. (1960). *The quest for certainty: A study of the relation of knowledge and action*. New York: Putnam (Original work published 1929).

Dewey, J. (2004). *Reconstruction in philosophy*. Mineola, NY: Dover Publications (Original work published 1920).

Dingle, H. (1950). A theory of measurement. *The British Journal for the Philosophy of Science, 1*(1), 5–26.

Domingue, B. (2014). Evaluating the equal-interval hypothesis with test score scales. *Psychometrika, 79*(1), 1–19.

Duncan, O. D. (1984). *Notes on social measurement: Historical and critical*. New York: Russell Sage Foundation.

Elmes, D. G., Kantowitz, B. H., & Roediger, H. L. (2012). *Research methods in psychology*. Melbourne: Wadsworth Cengage Learning.
Estes, W. (1975). Some targets for mathematical psychology. *Journal of Mathematical Psychology, 12*(3), 263–282.
Euclid. (1956). *The thirteen books of Euclid's Elements* (T. L. Heath, Trans.). New York: Dover Publications.
Falmagne, J.-C. (1976). Random conjoint measurement and loudness summation. *Psychological Review, 83*(1), 65–79.
Falmagne, J.-C. (1980). A probabilistic theory of extensive measurement. *Philosophy of Science, 47*(2), 277–296.
Finkelstein, L. (2003). Widely, strongly and weakly defined measurement. *Measurement, 34*(1), 39–48.
Formann, A. (1995). Linear logistic latent class analysis and the Rasch model. In G. H. Fischer & I. W. Molenaar (Eds.), *Rasch models: Foundations, recent developments, and applications* (pp. 239–256). New York: Springer-Verlag.
Franklin, W. (1903). Popular Science. *Science, 17*(418), 8–15.
Goodman, N. (1970). Seven strictures on similarity. In L. Foster & J. Swanson (Eds.), *Experience and Theory* (pp. 19–29). Amherst: University of Massachusetts Press.
Goodman, N. (1975). Words, works, worlds. *Erkenntnis*, 57–73.
Goodman, R. B. (1998). Wittgenstein and Pragmatism. *Parallax, 4*(4), 91–105.
Grace, R. C. (2001). On the failure of operationism. *Theory & Psychology, 11*(1), 5–33.
Green, C. D. (1992). Of immortal mythological beasts operationism in psychology. *Theory & Psychology, 2*(3), 291–320.
Green, C. D. (2001). Operationism again: What did Bridgman say? What did Bridgman need? *Theory & Psychology, 11*(1), 45–51.
Guilford, J. P. (1954). *Psychometric methods*. New York: McGraw-Hill.
Haack, R. (1982). Wittgenstein's pragmatism. *American Philosophical Quarterly, 19*(2), 163–171.
Haack, S. (1998). *Manifesto of a passionate moderate: unfashionable essays*. Chicago: University of Chicago Press.
Hacking, I. (2007). On not being a pragmatist: Eight reasons and a cause. In *New pragmatists* (pp. 32–49). New York: Oxford University Press.
Hagenaars, J. A., & McCutcheon, A. L. (2002). *Applied latent class analysis*. New York: Cambridge University Press.
Hand, D. J. (2004). *Measurement theory and practice*. London: Arnold.
Heinen, T. (1996). *Latent class and discrete latent trait models: Similarities and differences*. Thousand Oaks, CA: Sage.
Hensley, J. M. (2009). Who's Calling Wittgenstein a Pragmatist? *European Journal of Pragmatism and American Philosophy, 4*(2), 27–35.
Hölder, O. (1901). Die Axiome der Quantität und die Lehre vom Mass [The axioms of quantity and the theory of measurement]. In *Berichte über die Verhandlungen der Königlich-Sächsischen Gesellschaft der Wissenschaften zu Leipzig: Mathematische-Physische Classe* [Reports of the Proceedings of the Royal Saxon Society of Sciences in Leipzig: Mathematical-Physical Division] (Vol. 53, pp. 3–64).
Hood, B. (2009). Validity in psychological testing and scientific realism. *Theory and Psychology, 19*, 451–473.
Hornstein, G. A. (1988). Quantifying psychological phenomena: Debates, dilemmas, and implications. In J. G. Morawski (Ed.), *The rise of experimentation in american psychology* (pp. 1–34). New Haven: Yale University Press.
Huntington, E. V. (1902). A complete set of postulates for the theory of absolute continuous magnitude. *Transactions of the American Mathematical Society, 3*(2), 264–279.
Hutchins, E. (2000). *Cognition in the wild*. Cambridge, MA: The MIT Press.
International Measurement Confederation. (2014). *Table of Technical Committees*. Retrieved October 12, 2014, from http://www.imeko.org

James, W. (1907/1995). *Pragmatism*. New York: Dover Publications (Original work published 1907).

Johnson, H. M. (1936). Pseudo-mathematics in the mental and social sciences. *The American Journal of Psychology, 48*(2), 342–351.

Joint Committee for Guides in Metrology. (2008). *Evaluation of measurement data — Guide to the expression of uncertainty in measurement*. Paris: Bureau International des Poids et Mesures.

Joint Committee for Guides in Metrology. (2012). *The international vocabulary of metrology – Basic and general concepts and associated terms (VIM)* (3rd ed.). Paris: Bureau International des Poids et Mesures.

Kaarls, R. (2007). *Evolving needs for metrology in trade, industry and society and the role of the BIPM*. Paris: Bureau International des Poids et Mesures.

Knapp, T. R., & Mueller, R. O. (2010). Reliability and validity of instruments. In G. R. Hancock & R. O. Mueller (Eds.), *The reviewer's guide to quantitative methods in the social sciences* (pp. 337–341). New York, NY: Routledge.

Koch, S. (1992). Psychology's Bridgman vs Bridgman's Bridgman: An essay in reconstruction. *Theory and Psychology, 2*(3), 261–290.

Krantz, D. H. (1967). Extensive measurement in semiorders. *Philosophy of Science, 34*(4), 348–362.

Krantz, D. H., Luce, R. D., Suppes, P., & Tversky, A. (2007). *Foundations of measurement. Volume I: Additive and polynomial representations*. Mineola, NY: Dover Publications Inc. (Original work published 1971).

Kuhn, T. S. (1961). The function of measurement in modern physical science. *ISIS, 52*(2), 161–193.

Lakoff, G., & Johnson, M. (1999). *Philosophy in the flesh: The embodied mind and its challenge to Western thought*. New York: Basic Books.

Langeheine, R., & Rost, J. (1988). *Latent trait and latent class models*. New York: Plenum Press.

Laurence, S., & Margolis, E. (1999). Concepts and cognitive science. In E. Margolis & S. Laurence (Eds.), *Concepts: Core readings* (pp. 3–81). Cambridge, MA: MIT Press.

Lazarsfeld, P. F. (1961). Notes on the history of quantification in sociology – Trends, sources and problems. In H. Woolf (Ed.), *Quantification: A history of the meaning measurement in the natural and social sciences* (pp. 147–203). Indianapolis: Bobbs-Merrill.

Lazarsfeld, P. F., & Henry, N. W. (1968). *Latent structure analysis*. Boston: Houghton Mifflin Company.

Lindquist, E. F., & Thorndike, R. L. (Eds.). (1951). *Educational measurement*. Washington: American Council on Education.

Lord, F. M., & Novick, M. R. (1968). *Statistical theories of mental test scores*. Reading, MA: Addison-Wesley Pub. Co.

Lubke, G., & Muthen, B. O. (2005). Investigating population heterogeneity with factor mixture models. *Psychological Methods, 10*(1), 21–39.

Luce, R. D. (1956). Semiorders and a theory of utility discrimination. *Econometrica, 24*(2), 178–191.

Luce, R. D., Krantz, D. H., Suppes, P., & Tversky, A. (2007). *Foundations of measurement. Volume III*. Mineola, NY: Dover Publications Inc. (Original work published 1990).

Luce, R. D., & Suppes, P. (2002). Representational measurement theory. In H. Pashler & J. Wixted (Eds.), *Stevens' handbook of experimental psychology* (Vol. 4, pp. 1–41). New York: John Wiley and Sons.

Luce, R. D., & Tukey, J. W. (1964). Simultaneous conjoint measurement: A new type of fundamental measurement. *Journal of Mathematical Psychology, 1*(1), 1–27.

Margolis, E., & Laurence, S. (2014). Concepts. Retrieved October 12, 2014, from http://plato.stanford.edu/archives/spr2014/entries/concepts/

Margolis, J. (2009). A philosophical bestiary. *European Journal of Pragmatism & American Philosophy, 4*(2), 128–145.

Mari, L. (2000). Beyond the representational viewpoint: A new formalization of measurement. *Measurement, 27*(2), 71–84.

Mari, L. (2003). Epistemology of measurement. *Measurement, 34*(1), 17–30.
Mari, L. (2013). A quest for the definition of measurement. *Measurement, 46*(8), 2889–2895.
Mari, L. (2014). Evolution of 30 years of the International Vocabulary of Metrology (VIM). *Metrologia, 52*(1), R1–R10.
Markus, K. A., & Borsboom, D. (2013). *Frontiers of test validity theory: Measurement, causation and meaning*. New York: Routledge.
Maul, A. (2014). Justification is not truth, and testing is not measurement: Understanding the purpose and limitations of the standards. *Educational Measurement: Issues and Practice, 33*(4), 39–41.
McDonald, R. P. (1999). *Test theory a unified treatment*. Mahwah, NJ: Lawrence Erlbaum Associates.
Medin, D. L. (1989). Concepts and conceptual structure. *American Psychologist, 44*(12), 1469–1481.
Menand, L. (2001). *The metaphysical club*. New York: Farrar, Straus, and Giroux.
Messick, S. (1989). Validity. In R. Linn (Ed.), *Educational measurement* (pp. 13–104). New York, NY: Macmillan Publishing Company.
Michell, J. (1990). *An introduction to the logic of psychological measurement*. Hillsdale, NJ: Lawrence Erlbaum Associates, Inc.
Michell, J. (1993). The origins of the representational theory of measurement: Helmholtz, Hölder, and Russell. *Studies in History and Philosophy of Science Part A, 24*(2), 185–206.
Michell, J. (1997a). Bertrand Russell's 1897 critique of the traditional theory of measurement. *Synthese, 110*(2), 257–276.
Michell, J. (1997b). Quantitative science and the definition of measurement in psychology. *British Journal of Psychology, 88*(3), 355–383.
Michell, J. (1999). *Measurement in psychology: Critical history of a methodological concept*. New York: Cambridge University Press.
Michell, J. (2003). Pragmatism, positivism and the quantitative imperative. *Theory & Psychology, 13*(1), 45–52.
Michell, J. (2005). The logic of measurement: A realist overview. *Measurement, 38*(4), 285–294.
Michell, J. (2008a). Is psychometrics pathological science? *Measurement: Interdisciplinary Research & Perspective, 6*(1), 7–24.
Michell, J. (2008b). The measure of psychometrics — Review: Denny Borsboom, measuring the mind: Conceptual issues in contemporary psychometrics. *Theory & Psychology, 18*(1), 135–137.
Michell, J. (2011). Qualitative research meets the ghost of Pythagoras. *Theory & Psychology, 21*(2), 241–259.
Michell, J. (2012a). "The constantly recurring argument": Inferring quantity from order. *Theory and Psychology, 22*(3), 255–271.
Michell, J. (2012b). Alfred Binet and the concept of heterogeneous orders. *Frontiers in psychology, 3*(261), 1–8.
Michell, J. (2020). Thorndike's credo: Metaphysics in psychometrics. *Theory & Psychology, 30*(3), 309–328.
Michell, J., & Ernst, C. (1996). The axioms of quantity and the theory of measurement: Translated from Part I of Otto Hölder's German text "Die Axiome der Quantität und die Lehre vom Mass". *Journal of Mathematical Psychology, 40*(3), 235–252.
Michell, J., & Ernst, C. (1997). The axioms of quantity and the theory of measurement: Translated from Part II of Otto Hölder's German text "Die Axiome der Quantität und die Lehre vom Mass". *Journal of Mathematical Psychology, 41*(4), 345–356.
Minsky, M. (1968). Matter, Mind and Models. In M. Minsky (Ed.), *Semantic Information Processing* (pp. 425–432). Cambridge, MA: MIT Press.
Misak, C. J. (2013). *The American pragmatists*. Oxford: Oxford University Press.
Mislevy, R. J., & Haertel, G. (2006). Implications of evidence centered design for educational testing. *Educational Measurement: Issues and Practice, 25*(4), 6–20.

Muthen, B. O., & Asparouhov, T. (2006). Item response mixture modeling: Application to tobacco dependence criteria. *Addictive Behaviors, 31*(6), 1050–1066.
Nagel, E. (1931). Measurement. *Erkenntnis, 2*(1), 313–333.
Narens, L. (2013). *Introduction to the theories of measurement and meaningfulness and the use of symmetry in science*. Hove: Psychology Press.
Narens, L., & Luce, R. D. (1986). Measurement: The theory of numerical assignments. *Psychological Bulletin, 99*(2), 166–180.
Narens, L., & Luce, R. D. (1993). Further comments on the "nonrevolution" arising from axiomatic measurement theory. *Psychological Science, 4*(2), 127–130.
Nature Publishing Group. (1939). Quantitative estimates of sensory events. *Nature, 144*(3658), 973–973.
Nestor, P. G., & Schutt, R. K. (2014). *Research methods in psychology: Investigating human behavior*. Thousand Oaks, CA: Sage Publications.
Neurath, O. (1973). Anti-Spengler. In M. Neurath & R. S. Cohen (Eds.), *Empiricism and sociology* (pp. 158–213). Dordrecht, Holland: D. Reidel Publishing Company.
Núñez, R. E., & Freeman, W. J. (Eds.). (1999). *Reclaiming cognition: The primacy of action, intention, and emotion*. Thorverton: Imprint Academic.
Peirce, C. S. (1868). Some consequences of four incapacities. *The Journal of Speculative Philosophy, 2*(3), 140–157.
Peirce, C. S. (2014). How to make our ideas clear. In J. Buchler (Ed.), *Philosophical writings of Peirce* (pp. 23–41). New York: Dover Publications (Original work published 1878).
Perline, R., Wright, B. D., & Wainer, H. (1979). The Rasch model as additive conjoint measurement. *Applied Psychological Measurement, 3*(2), 237–255.
Pfanzagl, J. (1968). *Theory of measurement*. New York: Wiley.
Porter, T. M. (1996). *Trust in numbers: The pursuit of objectivity in science and public life*. Princeton University Press.
Psychometric Society. (2021). Psychometrics & the Psychometric Society. Retrieved October 14, 2014, from https://www.psychometricsociety.org/about-us
Putnam, H. (1995). *Pragmatism: An open question*. Cambridge, MA: Blackwell Publishers Inc.
Rasch, G. (1960/1980). *Probabilistic models for some intelligence and attainment tests*. Chicago: University of Chicago Press (Original work published 1960).
Rescher, N. (2007). Pragmatism. In C. V. Boundas (Ed.), *Columbia companion to twentieth-century philosophies* (pp. 128–142). New York: Columbia University Press.
Rorty, R. (1979). *Philosophy and the mirror of nature*. Princeton: Princeton University Press.
Rorty, R. (1982). *Consequences of pragmatism: Essays, 1972–1980*. Minneapolis: University of Minnesota Press.
Rorty, R. (1999). *Philosophy and social hope*. London: Penguin.
Rosch, E. (1978). Principles of categorization. In E. Rosch & B. Lloyd (Eds.), *Cognition and categorization* (pp. 24–78). Hilldate, NJ: Lawrence Erlbaum.
Rosch, E. (1999). Reclaiming concepts. *Journal of Consciousness Studies*, 6(11–12), 61–77.
Rosch, E., & Lloyd, B. (1978). *Cognition and categorization*. Hillsdale, NJ: Lawrence Erlbaum Associates.
Rosch, E., & Mervis, C. B. (1975). Family resemblances: Studies in the internal structure of categories. *Cognitive Psychology, 7*(4), 573–605.
Russell, B. (1897). On the Relations of Number and Quantity. *Mind, 6*(23), 326–341.
Russell, B. (1903). *The principles of mathematics, vol. 1*. Cambridge: University Press.
Savage, C. W. (1970). *The measurement of sensation: A critique of perceptual psychophysics*. Berkeley: University of California Press.
Schönemann, P. H. (1994). Measurement: The reasonable ineffectiveness of mathematics in the social sciences. *Trends and Perspectives in Empirical Social Research*, 149–160.
Schwager, K. W. (1991). The representational theory of measurement: An assessment. *Psychological Bulletin, 110*(3), 618–626.
Scott, D., & Suppes, P. (1958). Foundational aspects of theories of measurement. *Journal of Symbolic Logic, 23*(2), 113–128.

Sellars, W. (1956). Empiricism and the philosophy of mind. In Feigl & M. Scriven (Eds.), *Minnesota studies in the philosophy of science* (Vol. I, pp. 253–329). Minneapolis, MN: University of Minnesota Press.

Shanon, B. (1993). *The representational and the presentational: An essay on cognition and the study of mind*. London: Harvester Wheatsheaf.

Sherry, D. (2011). Thermoscopes, thermometers, and the foundations of measurement. *Studies in History and Philosophy of Science Part A, 42*(4), 509–524.

Skrondal, A., & Rabe-Hesketh, S. (2004). *Generalized latent variable modeling: Multilevel, longitudinal, and structural equation models*. Boca Raton, FL: Chapman & Hall/CRC.

Spearman, C. (1904a). "General Intelligence," objectively determined and measured. *The American Journal of Psychology, 15*(2), 201–292.

Spearman, C. (1904b). The proof and measurement of association between two things. *The American Journal of Psychology, 15*(1), 72–101.

Speitel, K. (1992). Measurement assurance. In G. Salvendy (Ed.), *Handbook of industrial engineering* (pp. 2235–2251). New York: Wiley.

Spengler, J. J. (1961). On the progress of quantification in economics. In H. Woolf (Ed.), *Quantification: A history of the meaning measurement in the natural and social sciences* (pp. 128–146). Indianapolis: Bobbs-Merrill.

Stevens, S. S. (1946). On the theory of scales of measurement. *Science, 103*(2684), 677–680.

Stevens, S. S. (1958). Measurement and man. *Science, 127*(3295), 383–389.

Suppes, P., Krantz, D. H., Luce, R. D., & Tversky, A. (2007). *Foundations of measurement. Volume II*. Mineola, NY: Dover Publications Inc. (Original work published 1989).

Suppes, P., & Zinnes, J. L. (1962). *Basic Measurement Theory* (tech. rep. No. 45). Institute for Mathematical Studies in the Social Sciences - Stanford University. Stanford, California.

Suppes, P., & Zinnes, J. L. (1963). Basic measurement theory. In R. D. Luce, R. Bush, & E. Galanter (Eds.), *Handbook of mathematical psychology, vol. 1* (pp. 3–76). New York: Wiley.

Tal, E. (2013). Old and new problems in philosophy of measurement. *Philosophy Compass, 8*(12), 1159–1173.

Tal, E. (2015). *Measurement in Science*. Retrieved July 28, 2015, from http://plato.stanford.edu/entries/measurement-science/

Tarpey, T. (2009). *All Models are Right... most are useless*. http://andrewgelman.com/wp-content/uploads/2012/03/tarpey.pdf

Tartaglia, J. (2007). *Routledge philosophy guidebook to Rorty and the mirror of nature*. London, New York: Routledge.

Teller, P. (2001). Twilight of the perfect model model. *Erkenntnis, 55*(3), 393–415.

Torgerson, W. S. (1958). *Theory and methods of scaling*. New York, NY: Wiley.

Trendler, G. (2009). Measurement theory, psychology and the revolution that cannot happen. *Theory and Psychology, 19*(5), 579–599.

Trout, J. D. (1998). *Measuring the intentional world realism, naturalism, and quantitative methods in the behavioral sciences*. New York: Oxford University Press.

Uebersax, J. (1993). Statistical modeling of expert ratings on medical treatment appropriateness. *Journal of the American Statistical Association, 88*(422), 421–427.

van der Linden, W. J. (1994). Fundamental measurement and the fundamentals of Rasch measurement. In M. Wilson (Ed.), *Objective measurement: Theory into practice* (Vol. 2, pp. 3–24). Norwood, NJ: Ablex Pub. Corp.

Van Fraassen, B. C. (2008). *Scientific representation: Paradoxes of perspective*. New York: Oxford University Press.

Van Onna, M. (2004). *Ordered latent class models in nonparametric item response theory* (Unpublished doctoral dissertation). University of Groningen, The Netherlands.

Varela, F. J., Thompson, E., & Rosch, E. (1991). *The embodied mind: Cognitive science and human experience*. Cambridge, MA: MIT Press.

Velleman, P. F., & Wilkinson, L. (1993). Nominal, ordinal, interval, and ratio typologies are misleading. *The American Statistician, 47*(1), 65–72.

Weitzenhoffer, A. M. (1951). Mathematical structures and psychological measurements. *Psychometrika, 16*(4), 387–406.

Westbrook, R. (2008). The pragmatist family romance. In C. Misak (Ed.), *The Oxford handbook of American philosophy* (pp. 185–196). Oxford: Oxford University Press.

Wigner, E. P. (1960). The unreasonable effectiveness of mathematics in the natural sciences. *Communications on Pure and Applied Mathematics, 13*(1), 1–14.

Wilson, M. (2005). *Constructing measures: An item response modeling approach*. Mahwah, NJ: Lawrence Erlbaum Associates.

Wilson, M. (2013). Using the concept of a measurement system to characterize measurement models used in psychometrics. *Measurement, 46*(9), 3766–3774.

Wittgenstein, L. (1965). *Preliminary studies for the "Philosophical investigations", generally know as the Blue and Brown books*. New York: Harper and Row.

Wittgenstein, L. (2003). *Philosophical investigations: The German text, with a Revised English translation* (G. E. M. Anscombe, Trans.). Malden, MA: Blackwell Publishing (Original work published 1953).

Wolins, L. (1978). Interval measurement: Physics, psychophysics, and metaphysics. *Educational and Psychological Measurement, 38*(1), 1–9.

Woolf, H. (Ed.). (1961). *Quantification: A history of the meaning measurement in the natural and social sciences*. Indianapolis: Bobbs-Merrill.

Wright, B. D. (1997). A history of social science measurement. *Educational measurement: Issues and practice, 16*(4), 33–45.

Index

D. Torres Irribarra, *A Pragmatic Perspective of Measurement*, SpringerBriefs in Psychology, https://doi.org/10.1007/978-3-030-74025-2

GPSR Compliance
The European Union's (EU) General Product Safety Regulation (GPSR) is a set of rules that requires consumer products to be safe and our obligations to ensure this.

If you have any concerns about our products, you can contact us on

ProductSafety@springernature.com

In case Publisher is established outside the EU, the EU authorized representative is:

Springer Nature Customer Service Center GmbH
Europaplatz 3
69115 Heidelberg, Germany

www.ingramcontent.com/pod-product-compliance
Ingram Content Group UK Ltd.
Pitfield, Milton Keynes, MK11 3LW, UK
UKHW020150290926
15471UKWH00004B/791
9783030740245